The Pullen Expedition

The Pullen Expedition

IN SEARCH OF SIR JOHN FRANKLIN

HAS BEEN PUBLISHED IN AN EDITION

OF 1,000 COPIES ONLY, OF WHICH

THIS IS COPY NUMBER

619

The Pullen Expedition

IN SEARCH OF SIR JOHN FRANKLIN

THE ORIGINAL DIARIES, LOG, AND LETTERS

OF COMMANDER W.J.S. PULLEN

SELECTED AND INTRODUCED BY H.F. PULLEN

O.B.E., C.D., Rear-Admiral, R.C.N. (Ret.)

THE ARCTIC HISTORY PRESS

The Arctic History Press,
18 Waterman Avenue,
Toronto, Ontario,
M4B 3G2

Pullen, William J.S., 1813–1887.
The Pullen Expedition in search of Sir John Franklin

Bibliography: p. 224
Includes index.

ISBN 0-7710-0335-8

1. Pullen, William J.S., 1813–1887.
2. Explorers Arctic regions–Biography.
3. Franklin, John, Sir, 1786–1847.
4. Arctic regions. I. Pullen, Hugh F., 1905–
II. Title.

G665 1848.P85   917.19′3′040924   C79-094125-2

To all those
who went in search of
Franklin,
1848–1859,
and in so doing
unlocked
the Canadian Arctic

Acknowledgements

This account of a little known boat expedition in the search for Sir John Franklin could not have been written without the help of a great many people. I have received much assistance in my search for information on many aspects of this expedition. Any mistakes or errors in the final presentation are my responsibility.

In particular I am most grateful to: Doctor O.M. Solandt, who has been kind enough to write the Foreword to this book; the Controller of H.M. Stationery Office for permission to publish facsimiles of Crown copyright records in the Public Record Office; Mr. W.I. Smith, Dominion Archivist, Mr. C.C.J. Bond of the Map Division, and Mr. G. Delisle of the Picture Division, Public Archives of Canada, Ottawa, Ontario; Mrs. Shirlee A. Smith, the Librarian, and Miss Malvina Bolus, Editor of the *Beaver*, Hudson's Bay Company, Winnipeg, Manitoba; Mrs. J. Craig, the Archivist of the Hudson's Bay Company, London; Miss N.T. Corley, Librarian, The Arctic Institute of North America, Montreal, P.Q.; Mrs. Georgina Barrass, Assistant Archivist, Glenbow-Alberta Institute, Calgary, Alberta; Mr. T.F. Bredin, Fort Garry, Winnipeg, Manitoba; Mr. J.A. Bovey, Provincial Archivist, Winnipeg, Manitoba; Miss Shirley Elliott, Librarian, Legislative Library, Halifax, Nova Scotia; Commander W.H. Fowler, C.D., R.C.N. (Ret.), Kentville, Nova Scotia; Miss Pamela A. Hardisty, Assistant Librarian, Library of Parliament, Ottawa, Ontario; the Trustees of the British Museum, London; the Hydrographer of the Navy, Hydrographic Department, Taunton, Somerset; Mr. M.W.B. Sanderson, Librarian, National Maritime Museum, Greenwich; Major General N. Elliott Rodger, C.B.E., C.D., Winnipeg, Manitoba; E.W. Morse, Esq., Ottawa, Ontario; Mr. A.O. Anderson, Washington, D.C., U.S.A.; the Very Rev. D.A. Ford, B.A., B.D., Saskatoon, Saskatchewan; the Rev. Canon J.D.F. Beattie, M.A., B.D., D.D., Saskatoon, Saskatchewan; the Rev. Canon D.W. Roberts, Killarney, Manitoba; the Rev. J. Ivey, The Pas, Manitoba; Professor J. Ross Mackay, University of British Columbia, Vancouver, British Columbia; Associate Professor J.K. Seager, University of British Columbia, Vancouver, British Columbia; the late Mr. O.B. McAdoo, H.M.C. Chart and Chronometer Depot, H.M.C. Dockyard, Halifax, Nova Scotia; Mrs. M.E. Clarke, Montreal, P.Q.

Contents

Maps and Illustrations

A Chronology of
the Franklin Searches

1845-48 Captain Sir John Franklin and Captain F.R.M. Crozier in H.M. Ships *Erebus* and *Terror*.

1846-47 Dr. John Rae, boat expedition from York Factory.

1847-49 Sir John Richardson and Dr. Rae, overland and by boat.

1848-49 Captain Sir J.C. Ross and Captain E.J. Bird in H.M. Ships *Enterprise* and *Investigator*.

1849-50 Commander James Saunders in H.M.S. *North Star*.

1849-50 Lieutenant W.J.S. Pullen and Mr. W.H. Hooper, acting Mate with two boats from H.M.S. *Plover*.

1849 Several whaling ships assist in the search.

1850-51 Captain H.T. Austin, Captain E. Ommaney, Lieutenant S. Osborn and Lieutenant B. Cator in H.M. Ships *Resolute, Assistance, Intrepid* and *Pioneer*.

1850-51 Captain W. Penny and Captain A. Stewart in the *Lady Franklin* and *Sophia*.

1850-51 Lieutenant E.J. DeHaven, U.S.N., and Mr. S.P. Griffin in the ships *Advance* and *Rescue* (private United States expedition.)

1850-51   Commander Sir John Ross and Commander G. Phillips in the *Felix* and yacht *Mary*, private expedition.

1850   Captain C.C. Forsyth in the *Prince Albert*, private expedition.

1850-55   Captain R. Collinson in H.M.S. *Enterprise*.

1850-54   Captain R.leM. McClure in H.M.S. *Investigator*.

1850-51   Dr. John Rae, overland and by boat.

1851-52   Commander W. Kennedy and Lieutenant J.R. Bellot, French Navy, in the *Prince Albert*, private expedition.

1852   Commander E.A. Inglefield in the steam vessel *Isabel*, private expedition.

1852-54   Captain Sir Edward Belcher and Lieutenant S. Osborn in H.M. Ships *Assistance* and *Pioneer*.

1852-54   Captain H. Kellett and Commander F.L. M'Clintock in H.M. Ships *Resolute* and *Intrepid*.

1852-54   Commander W.J.S. Pullen in H.M.S. *North Star*, base ship for the Belcher expedition.

1853   Captain E.A. Inglefield and Mr. W.H. Fawckner in H.M.S. *Phoenix* and the transport *Breadalbane*.

1853-54   Dr. John Rae by boat and overland.

1853-55   Dr. E.K. Kane in the *Advance*, private United States expedition.

1855   James Anderson and J.G. Stewart, Hudson's Bay Company expedition by canoe.

1857-59   Captain F.L. M'Clintock in the *Fox*, private expedition, which found remains of the Franklin expedition.

Foreword

It is particularly appropriate that this story of the competent and courageous conduct of a very important part of the Franklin Search by Commander W.J.S. Pullen of the Royal Navy should be brought to public attention by his descendant, Rear Admiral Hugh Pullen of the Royal Canadian Navy. With the characteristic understatement of naval men everywhere, Commander Pullen has told a simple and unembroidered tale, and the Admiral has added just enough to set this great adventure in context. Although the voyage was a very important part of the Franklin Search, since it covered in detail a part of the coastline that Franklin and his party might well have reached, the full account of it has not before been generally available and it is only mentioned in passing in larger works on the Franklin Searches. It probably did not attract much attention because the number of people involved was small; the voyage that was planned was completed according to plan; no trace of Franklin's party was found, and, most important of all, Commander Pullen and his entire party came through alive and in reasonably good health. Had their voyage ended in disaster, their story would probably be known to every schoolboy.

Anyone who is at all familiar with the North, either through personal contact or vicariously by reading the works of other explorers, will know that this was no picnic. The very great hardships of being frequently wet and usually cold with what we would now consider to be most inadequate food and clothing, terribly long hours at sea without any rest and when ashore continuous anxiety over the attitude of the Eskimos, must have made it a most wearing experience. Little of this shows directly in Commander Pullen's simple and gripping narrative.

Appendix 8, which is a letter from Dr. Rae to Sir John Richardson from Fort Simpson, 5 October 1849, carries this understatement to its logical conclusion. He says, "The seamen are almost completely naked; they left the ship without any other clothes but those they had on their backs and none of the party had a blanket or a substitute for one. Providentially they had fine weather and consequently did not suffer much inconvenience."

The second voyage in the summer of 1850 was very limited because of the unusually bad ice conditions that were encountered. Probably the poor condition of the boats contributed to the lack of progress. Nonetheless, the two Arctic voyages, together with the return by the Fur Trade Route to York Factory, comprise a tale of great courage, determination and competence which adds an important chapter both to the history of the Royal Navy and to the story of the pioneers who made Canada.

O.M. Solandt.

Preface

This is an account of one of the first expeditions that went in search of Sir John Franklin and his men. In 1847, the Admiralty organized three such undertakings, which were to start the following year. One was to enter Lancaster Sound and "follow" the missing ships. A second one, in open boats, was to explore the coast from Point Barrow to the Mackenzie River, while a third would carry out a similar task from the Mackenzie to the Coppermine River. This narrative has to do with the search from Point Barrow, eastward to the Mackenzie. Despite great hardship and considerable difficulty with ice and shallow water, no trace was found of the Franklin expedition.

This particular boat expedition, which is one of the least known of the Franklin searches, was commanded by Commander W.J.S. Pullen, R.N. His official reports are to be found in the "House of Commons' command papers relating to the Franklin Search Expeditions." There is also some reference to it in *Arctic Expeditions. . . .* by D. Murray Smith, and in W.H. Hooper's *Ten Months among the Tents of the Tuski*. In 1934 I was shown an account of this expedition, written by W.J.S. Pullen in 1882, and which I was allowed to copy. This was used as the basis for an article in the *Scottish Geographical Magazine* of July 1935. It also appeared in *The Beaver* for March and June 1947. The only other reference I have found is in the Hudson's Bay Record Society's volume, *Rae's Arctic Correspondence, 1844-55*.

For many years I have felt that this boat expedition should be better known, and as a result I have been collecting what information I could find. Here are the official reports, written by Commander Pullen, often under very difficult and trying conditions. They tell a story of courage, fortitude and resolution in the face of great hardship, isolation, bitter weather and hazardous conditions of ice and shoal water. While no trace was found of Franklin, the expedition did establish the fact that he was not to the westward of Cape Bathurst.

There is a fascination about these missing ships, and the tragic fate of their officers and men, even though it all happened over one hundred and thirty years ago. Many brave men and many ships were involved in the search. Their efforts were directly responsible for much discovery and exploration, that led to a greatly increased knowledge of the North. Canada owes much to all those who went in search of Franklin.

H.F.P.
Big Hill,
Chester Basin,
Nova Scotia.

Prologue

From England to the Arctic
17 May 1848 to 15 July 1849

On 19 May 1845, Captain Sir John Franklin, K.C.B., R.N., sailed from the Thames in command of H.M.S. *Erebus*, with H.M.S. *Terror*, Captain Francis Rawdon Moirs Crozier, R.N., in company. These two ships had been specially prepared for Arctic service, and were stored and provisioned for three years. They were manned by one hundred and twenty-nine officers and men. Franklin's orders from the Admiralty were to enter Lancaster Sound, and proceed as far west in Barrow Strait as the "longitude of that portion of land on which Cape Walker is situated, or about 98 degrees west. From that point we desire that every effort be used to endeavour to penetrate to the southward and westward, in a course as direct towards Bhering's Strait as the position and extent of the ice, or the existence of land at present unknown, may admit."[1] This position off Cape Walker is at the northern tip of Prince of Wales Land, and the western end of Barrow Strait.

Early in 1847 there was great concern in Great Britain for the safety of the Franklin expedition. It had not been reported since sailing from Disco, on the west coast of Greenland, on 12 July 1845. H.M. Ships *Erebus* and *Terror* were last seen by the whaler *Prince of Wales* in Melville Bay on 26 July 1845, trying to work their way through or round the ice on their way into Lancaster Sound. As their mastheads disappeared below the horizon on that July day, they vanished from the sight of man, never to be seen again.

In view of the public concern, the Admiralty said that if nothing was heard of the Franklin expedition by the summer of 1847, three relief expeditions would be organized and sent off the following year.[2] The first one would consist of H.M.S. *Plover*, which was to act as a base ship for boat searching parties along the north coast from the vicinity of the Bering Strait to the Mackenzie River.[3] She sailed from Plymouth on 18 February 1848, and was to be joined by H.M.S. *Herald* in the summer of that year. The boat parties were instructed to try and make contact with Sir John Richardson's overland expedition.

The second expedition was made up of H.M. Ships *Enterprise*, Captain Sir James Clark Ross, R.N., and *Investigator*, Captain Edward Joseph Bird, R.N. They were to enter Lancaster Sound and "follow" the missing ships, making their way to Barrow Strait.[4] The *Enterprise* was to winter at Melville Island or Banks Land, while the *Investigator* was to find winter quarters near Cape Rennell, on the north coast of North Somerset Island. In 1849, parties from the *Enterprise* were to explore the west and east coasts of Banks Land, and then make their way to Cape Parry or Cape Bathurst, and then to Fort Good Hope on the Mackenzie River.

When the Admiralty was considering plans for the Franklin search, one of those consulted was Medical Inspector Sir John Richardson, M.D., of the Royal Naval Hospital at Haslar. He had been with Franklin in his two overland expeditions to the arctic coast of Canada in 1819-22, and 1825-27. Richardson offered a number of suggestions, one of which was a boat expedition along the coast from the Mackenzie to the Coppermine River, with visits being paid to Wollaston and Victoria Lands, before wintering at Fort Confidence on Great Bear Lake. His offer to lead this expedition was accepted by the Admiralty. This became the third Franklin search of 1848.[5]

The Admiralty issued the necessary orders to Sir John Richardson,[6] at the same time making arrangements to have four specially designed boats built, suitable men selected for their crews, and the stores, provisions and instruments collected.[7]

Five seamen of the Royal Navy and fifteen men of the Corps of Royal Sappers and Miners volunteered and were selected.[8] They, together with the boats and stores, sailed from Gravesend on 15 June 1847, on board the Hudson's Bay Company ships *Prince Rupert*, Captain D.G. Heard, and *Westminster*, Captain Forbes Michie, arriving at York Factory on the 25th and 30th August respectively.[9] Here they were met by Mr. John Bell, Chief Trader of the Hudson's Bay Company, who had been appointed to take charge of the expedition until Sir John Richardson was available. This was an unusual situation with a civilian in charge of military personnel.[10] In the case of the sappers and miners, before sailing from England all had signed a document in which they stated that they "bind and oblige themselves to perform the duties of the said expedition in obedience to the said Sir John Richardson and the other officers, and also to follow the directions of Chief Trader John Bell, or other superior officers of the Hudson's Bay Company, who may be entrusted with the direction of the expedition until it is joined by Sir John Richardson. ..."[11]

This small party of naval and military volunteers was seen by Dr. Rae when he arrived at York Factory from Repulse Bay on 6 September, at the conclusion of his first Arctic expedition of 1846-47. Mr. Bell took charge of these men, with their boats and stores, and other paraphernalia, and set off for Cumberland House on the Saskatchewan River, where they spent the winter of 1847-48.

Dr. Rae sailed for England where he arrived in late October 1847. From the manner in which he had carried out his expedition, it was quite clear that he was a skilful and capable Arctic explorer. Sir John Richardson asked the Admiralty to obtain his services from the Hudson's Bay Company. A request was made by letter on 16 December to which the Hudson's Bay Company made a favourable reply on the 28th, and Rae became the second in command of Richardson's expedition in the search for Franklin.[12]

Both men sailed from Liverpool on board the British and

North American Royal Mail Steam Packet Company's ship
Hibernia, on 25 March 1848, and arrived at New York on 10
April. They reached Montreal on the 15th, and after spending a
few days with Sir George Simpson at his headquarters at
Lachine, set off to join Mr. Bell and his party somewhere along
the route to the Mackenzie River. Travelling by steamer, they
reached Sault Ste. Marie on the 29th, embarked in two "north
canoes",[13] and by 4 May were on their way to Fort William,
where they arrived on the 12th, after skirting the north shore of
Lake Superior. By 5 June they were at Norway House, and eight
days later had arrived at Cumberland House. They finally
caught up with Mr. Bell at the Methy Portage on the 28th.

According to Richardson's account of this journey half way
across North America, the distance from New York to Sault Ste.
Marie, via Lachine, Buffalo and Detroit, was about fifteen hundred miles, which was covered by river and lake steamer. From
Sault Ste. Marie to Cumberland House he and Dr. Rae in two
express "north canoes" travelled another 1388 miles in forty-one
days, averaging about thirty-four miles per day. From Cumberland House, which they left early on 14 June, until they reached
the portage at the upper end of Methy Lake on the evening of
the 28th, they travelled another six hundred miles in fourteen
days, at about forty-three miles per day. This entire journey was
a good example of the skill, speed and endurance of the voyag-
eurs, in express canoes with long hours of travel.

Nine days were spent in getting the stores and provisions
across the portage. It took two and a half days of this to get the
four boats transported on the men's shoulders. By the evening of
5 July everything was on the banks of the Clearwater River, and
the next morning Sir John Richardson and his expedition set off.
He with Dr. Rae and eighteen men and three boats reached
Fort Resolution on Great Slave Lake on the 17th, crossed it and
went down the Mackenzie River to the Beaufort Sea. Mr. Bell
and his party went on to Great Bear Lake, where they were to
rebuild Fort Confidence, which had been destroyed by fire.
Richardson's orders were to search the coast between the Mack-

enzie and Coppermine Rivers, depositing caches of pemmican at Point Separation, Cape Bathurst, Cape Parry, Cape Krusenstern and Fort Good Hope. If weather and time allowed, a search was to be made of the west and south coasts of Wollaston Land.

While *Erebus* and *Terror* were working their way across the North Atlantic in the early summer of 1845, far away to the southward, H.M.S. *Columbia*, Captain William Fitz William Owen, R.N., was engaged in surveying the Bay of Fundy. One of her officers was Lieutenant William John Samuel Pullen, R.N.[14] He had joined the *Columbia* in 1844, after several years exploring and surveying in South Australia, where he had met Lady Franklin. In the Royal Navy he and his two brothers were following in the footsteps of their father, both grandfathers and six uncles.

H.M.S. *Columbia* returned to England and was paid off at Chatham on 12 February 1848. On her way up the Channel she passed H.M.S. *Plover*, which had been fitted out at Sheerness for service in the Arctic and was on her way to Plymouth before sailing for the Bering Sea.[15] Just before the *Columbia* was paid off, each of the four junior lieutenants in the ship received a note from Rear Admiral Sir Francis Beaufort, the Hydrographer of the Navy (1829-55), asking if any one of them would accept an appointment as first lieutenant of *Plover*.

Pullen, who was a surveyor as well as being the junior lieutenant in the *Columbia*, had been sent to the Admiralty to return the charts and chronometers belonging to his ship. This was the usual custom or practice on a ship paying off. He arrived at the Admiralty on 14 February, and reported himself to the Hydrographer. On being shown into his office, Sir Francis asked if he would go out in the *Plover* as first lieutenant. She was due to sail for the Bering Strait on 18 February, to act as the base ship for a boat expedition in the search for Sir John Franklin.

In Pullen's words, "it was rather a startling question, especially as I had just paid off after a five year commission, and hardly knew how to get ready for such a service in so short a time."[16] Sir Francis left Pullen alone with his thoughts for a few minutes and, on his return, asked him if he would accept the appointment if the Admiralty sent him out to join the *Plover* at Panama. This would mean a passage by mail steamer, leaving England about mid-May. The *Plover* would be ordered to call at Panama on her way north from Cape Horn. Pullen agreed and, as he said in his account of this meeting with Sir Francis Beaufort, "off I went to Plymouth, where I found the *Plover*, to whom the Admiralty appointed a lieutenant till I should join her."[17]

H.M.S. *Plover*, Commander Thomas Edward Laws Moore, R.N.,[18] had sailed from Plymouth on 18 February 1848, bound for the Bering Strait by way of Cape Horn. She was to call at Panama for Lieutenant Pullen, and then proceed to a rendezvous off Chamisso Island in Kotzebue Sound. This is on the west coast of Alaska, north of the Bering Strait. Here she would be joined by H.M.S. *Herald*, which was to supply her with stores and provisions. The *Plover* was to act as a base ship for boat parties that were to search the coast eastward towards the Mackenzie River.

Captain Henry Kellett, C.B., R.N., commissioned *Herald*, in 1845, to carry out a survey of the west coast of Central America, the Gulf of California and Vancouver Island. On 26 June 1845, she sailed from Plymouth, with H.M.S. *Pandora*, Lieutenant-Commander James Wood, R.N., in company. The *Pandora* was to act as a tender to the *Herald* in her surveying duties, and it was the *Pandora* that carried out the first survey of Esquimalt Harbour in 1846.

For two and a half years the *Herald* and the *Pandora* were busily engaged in their surveying duties. On 12 February 1848, they arrived at Panama, having "finished the delineation of the coast of Western South America."[19] Here Captain Kellett received a letter from the Admiralty, dated 13 December 1847,[20] instructing him to join forces with *Plover* in the Bering Strait, in the search for Franklin, and to communicate with Sir John Richardson on the Mackenzie River. Kellett wrote to the Admiralty on the 24th. to say that provisions were not available at Pana-

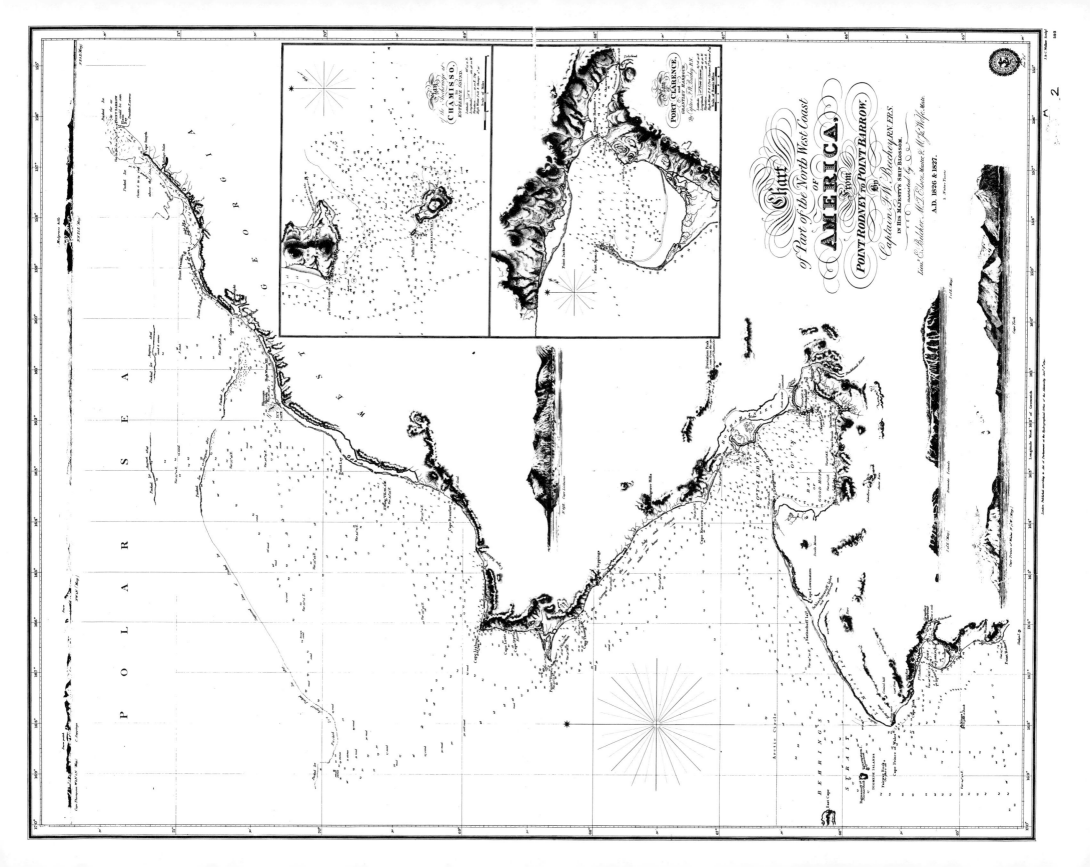

Chart
of Part of the North West Coast
of
AMERICA,
from
POINT RODNEY to POINT BARROW.
By
Captain F.W. Beechey. R.N. F.R.S.
IN HIS MAJESTY'S SHIP BLOSSOM.
assisted by
Lieut. E. Belcher, M.T. Elson, Master & M.J. Wolfe Mate.
A.D. 1826 & 1827.

Chart of
the Anchorage at
CHAMISSO,
in
KOTZEBUE SOUND.

Plan of
PORT CLARENCE,
and
GRANTLEY HARBOUR.
By Captain F.W. Beechey R.N.

POLAR SEA

WEST
GEORGIA

BEHRINGS STRAIT

Arctic Circle

ma, and that he had sent a copy of the Admiralty's instructions and a demand for provisions to the Commander-in-Chief, Pacific Station.[21] The *Herald* and the *Pandora* then sailed "to survey the coast westward of Punta Mala, the islands of Coyba and Quicara, and the approaches to Boca Chica."[22] They returned to Panama about the end of April 1848 and embarked their provisions. On 9 May, *Herald*, in tow of H.M.S. *Sampson*, left Panama, with *Pandora* in company. The *Herald* was towed about six hundred miles to the westward to pick up the trade winds. On the 11th. the *Pandora* was detached, with orders to meet the *Plover* at Oahu, and then proceed to the Straits of Juan de Fuca to finish the survey. Three days later the *Sampson* cast off the tow, but it was several days before the *Herald* found the trade winds.

On 17 May 1848, Lieutenant Pullen sailed from Southampton on board the West India mail steamer *Medway*, Captain W. Symonds, bound for Chagres on the Isthmus of Panama. He landed on 17 June, and crossed the Isthmus by "canoe and mule", on his way to Panama where he was to join the *Plover*. That ship, after rounding the Horn, called at Callao, and eventually arrived at Honolulu on 23 August 1848. According to Mr. W.H. Hooper, Acting Mate, R.N., and one of her officers, "the voyage" was "greatly protracted by calm and contrary winds, and the very indifferent sailing qualities of our vessel."[23] These indifferent sailing qualities were undoubtedly the reason why the *Plover* did not call at Panama. Pullen waited for her there until 27 July, when he was ordered to join *Asia*, wearing the flag of Rear-Admiral of the White Phipps-Hornby, C.B., Commander-in-Chief, Pacific Station. The *Asia*, which had some cases of smallpox on board, was lying at Payta in Northern Peru. Shortly after Pullen joined, she sailed for Valparaiso, and there he served until the spring of 1849.

The *Herald*, after leaving Panama on 9 May 1849, steered a course for Petropavlovsk, Kamtchatka, where she arrived on 7 August. She sailed again on the 14th. for the rendezvous with the *Plover* in Kotzebue Sound, where she arrived on 14 September. There was no sign of that vessel, though Captain Kellett waited until the 29th. for her. The *Plover* left Honolulu, complete with stores, provisions and water on 25 August, and worked her way slowly to the north west. She crossed the latitude of Attu Island (53°N), the westernmost island in the Aleutian chain, on 27 September, just two days before the *Herald* sailed from Kotzebue Sound. These two ships, having sailed thousands of miles, were not too far apart, but their means of communication were such that unless they sighted each other, they might just as well have been at the opposite ends of the earth.

On leaving Kotzebue Sound, the *Herald* proceeded to the southward to continue her surveying duties. The *Plover*, since sailing from Honolulu, had to struggle against head winds and adverse currents. She sighted St. Lawrence Island on 13 October, but was set to the south-westward, and was quite unable to make any progress towards the rendezvous in Kotzebue Sound. The season was getting late for a vessel to be at sea in those waters, so on 16 October, Commander Moore took his ship into a bay close to Cape Tchvkotsky, near the south-east point of Eastern Siberia, and there the *Plover* spent the winter of 1848-49. Moore called this place Emma Harbour; today it is known as Providence Bay. Here he and his officers and men made friends with the natives, refitted the ship, did some exploring, and got ready for the next season.

The plans made by the Admiralty to search the north coast of America during 1848, had failed, largely due to the poor sailing qualities of *Plover*. As the year ended, she was in winter quarters on the east coast of Siberia, the *Herald* was surveying on the west coast of North America, and Lieutenant Pullen was serving on board *Asia*, somewhere on the west coast of South America.

On 11 March 1849, Pullen embarked in a small brig called *Velocity*, a factor that had been missing from the Franklin search so far. This vessel had been chartered by the Commander-in-Chief to take stores, provisions and two whale boats to[24] the Sandwich Islands, where she was to meet the *Herald* and transfer the cargo to her. The *Velocity* anchored in Honolulu Harbour on 27 April 1849, and waited until 11 May, before the *Herald* arrived. It was now almost a year since Pullen had sailed from England, and he was still a long way from *Plover* and the Arctic coast of North America. The *Herald* embarked and, with Pullen on board, sailed on 19 May, to meet the *Plover* at the rendezvous off Chamisso Island in Kotzebue Sound.

While the *Herald* and *Velocity* were busy in mid-Pacific, the *Plover* was not being idle. Moore reported to the Admiralty that "in the beginning of April [1849], finding that the sea edge of the ice began to break away, I set about fitting the ship for sea, which was completed in the fine weather of that month, and on the 22nd. of May, when the floes had broken as far as the fetch of the sea would reach, I deemed it necessary to commence cutting the ship out of the remaining portion, which appeared fixed by two opposite points of land a mile and a quarter astern of the ship. The ice was found from five to six feet thick, and cutting out seemed a formidable operation for so small a crew; but the officers and men set to with such alacrity, and carried on with such perseverance, that, notwithstanding interruptions occasioned by snow storms, the work of cutting a canal of 2000 yards in length was completed in 22 days, and on the 13th. June I had the pleasure of seeing the *Plover* released from her icy cradle, and at anchor in the clear water of the harbour."[25] The ship was much delayed by drifting ice and contrary winds, but finally got to sea on 11 July, and anchored at the rendezvous off Chamisso Island on 14 July 1849.

On leaving Honolulu, the *Herald* proceeded to Petropaulovsk, where she anchored on 23 June. There was no sign or word of the *Plover*, but lying at anchor in Awachta Bay, near Petropaulovsk, was the schooner yacht *Nancy Dawson*, wearing the burgee of the Royal Thames Yacht Club. Her owner, Robert Shedden, who had been a mate in the Royal Navy, had brought his yacht out to help in the search for Franklin. Both ships sailed on 27 June, and the *Herald* anchored off Chamisso Island on 15 July. Here at last was the *Plover*.

The day the *Herald* arrived, Commander Moore had sent away the *Plover*'s pinnace with Lieutenant W.A.R. Lee, R.N., in

29

command. He was accompanied by the *Plover*'s gig, in charge of Mr. W.H. Hooper. Both boats were victualled for seventy days, and their orders were to proceed to the Mackenzie River, about a thousand miles away, along the north coast of America, looking for signs of Sir John Franklin and his party. Before the boats were out of sight, the *Herald* appeared and they were recalled.

Lieutenant Pullen finally joined the *Plover* on 15 July 1849, fourteen months after leaving England, and having travelled thousands of miles by steam and sailing ship, to say nothing of the canoe and even the humble mule.

As soon as the *Herald* had transferred the stores to the *Plover*, both ships sailed for Wainwright Inlet, examining the coast for a winter berth for the *Plover* as they proceeded. They left Kotzebue Sound on 18 July, and that afternoon were joined by the *Nancy Dawson*. All three ships anchored near Cape Lisburne on the 20th., and Pullen was sent away with two boats to examine the coast for a suitable berth. In this he was not successful. The ships continued their passage up the coast, and on 25 July anchored off Wainwright Inlet. It was Captain Kellett's intention to despatch the boat expedition from this position, as it was important that the officer in charge of the boats should know where the *Plover* was to spend the winter. If she was not to be found in Wainwright Inlet, she would be near Chamisso Island.

Chapter One

Wainwright Inlet to Fort Simpson, 25 July to 3 October 1849

Lieutenant W.J.S. Pullen, R.N., was put in charge of the boat expedition, and was given a most explicit set of orders by Commander Moore.[1] These were supplemented by further advice by Captain Kellett.[2] In general terms Pullen was to proceed to the Mackenzie River with his flotilla of boats. If the two large ones made progress slow and difficult, he was to send them back to Refuge Inlet. He was to keep close to the land so that he would not miss any marks that had been left by the Franklin party. On reaching Point Separation on the Mackenzie River in 67° 37′ North, 134° 05′ West, he was to leave information concerning his movements, location of provisions, and then return to the *Plover*. If he considered that this could not be done by 15 September, he was to make his way to one of the Hudson's Bay Company's posts on the Mackenzie to spend the winter. In due course he was to make his way to York Factory "reporting yourself and party to their Lordships with as little delay as possible."[3]

On board the *Herald* and *Plover* there was much activity in preparing the boats, collecting stores, provisions and equipment, and selecting the officers and men who were to take part in the expedition. This was no small undertaking, for they were to search the Arctic coast of North America in open boats. It was an audacious project, but quite within the capabilities of the Royal Navy. Captain Kellett's account, taken from his report of

33

proceedings, tells the story of the departure of the boat expedition.

"By midnight [25/26 July 1849] the boats were all ready, and shoved off under three hearty cheers from the ships, which were as heartily returned by the boats.

This little expedition consisted of 25 persons, and four boats, as follows: — Lieutenant Pullen, commanding the *Herald*'s 30 foot pinnace, fitted on board with the greatest care, thoroughly decked, schooner-rigged, and called the *Owen*, furnished with pumps, spare rudder, and a strengthening piece of two-inch plank above her water line.

Two 27 foot whale boats, new boats, brought out by Her Majesty's ship *Asia*, from England, covered in abaft as far as the backboard, but without either boxes or cases, the provisions being stowed, the bread in painted bags, and the preserved meats between tarpawlings. The men's clothing were in haversacks, capable of removal in a moment.

Plover's pinnace, a half-decked boat, with cases for her provisions, etc, so placed as to resist pressure from the ice.

There were placed in the boats 70 day's preserved meats for the whole party, all the other articles of provisions, except bread, to the same extent, being also soldered up in tins. In addition to these, the *Owen* had on board eight men's allowance of the regular ship's provisions. After she was stowed with this proportion, every corner that would hold a case of preserved meats was filled. The two larger boats carried in lack of them five cases of pemmican for the special use of Sir John Franklin's party.

The ships weighed in company with the boats, and ran along the land within about three miles, with a moderate off shore wind."[4]

The first reports from Lieutenant Pullen were contained in a private letter and an official one, both addressed to Captain Kellett, and delivered by the yacht *Nancy Dawson*. The private letter reads:

Schooner *Owen*, Monday Evening.
30 July, 1849.

Dear Sir,

We have got this far very well, may the rest of our expedition prove as successful. We hit the main pack in 71° 15′ 58″ N, much farther south than I at all expected, from the mildness of the weather and the fine open sea. I have been unsuccessful in my search for a place for the boats; not even Refuge Inlet, very shallow and a very narrow entrance.

If I do not get to Fort Good Hope, Captain Moore directs me to proceed to York Factory, provided there are not supplies there, and report myself to their Lordships, so it will rest with them whether I return next season much as I should like it. We have been detained here a day with a strong wind, and great quantities of ice completely blocking the Channel. Our whale boats are now loaded, and swim very deep, so I think I shall most likely take the larger boats on to Point Barrow, that is if possible.

We have had most beautiful weather till today and the thermometer was last night down to 36°. We have found the *Owen* rather leaky, but nothing to prevent our getting on. The pump is very good.

The latitude of the most southern part of the pack was 72° 15′ 48″ N, Mer Alt, and where we anchored formed a large bay with the shore, the outer or SE point of the pack being about two miles from the shore. The Channel is in the deep of this bay, close in there and very narrow.

In the bay are two small Ice Bergs, under the lee of one and close up to it (moored to it) we are now lying with the *Nancy Dawson*. I have seen several natives and rubbed noses with some again, not a pleasant situation I assure you.

Mr Shedden has promised to deliver these letters, and from him I have got a copy of reckoning, shewing his track, and now dear Sir I must close.

Captain Moore has got a full account of all I have done, with kind remembrances to all my messmates and ship-mates, and gratitude to you for your kind feelings, and acts of goodness.

Believe me to be,
Dear Sir,

Yours very truly,
(Sgd) W.J.S. Pullen.

Captain Kellett, C.B.
H.M.S. *Herald.*[5]

Lieutenant.

Pullen's official report to Captain Kellett reads:

"Schooner *Owen* fast under the lee of an ice berg, Pinnace and the two whale boats close along side, also schooner yacht *Nancy Dawson* in company.
Latitude 71° 15′ 56″ N, two miles off shore.

Monday, 30 July 1849.
Sir,

I beg to inform you of my anchoring with the boat at 3.15 yesterday afternoon at the edge of the pack, and the entrance of a narrow Channel leading Northward close along shore. We have had a long passage up, but towing two boats in the wind, light sometimes, and always foul, has been the cause. The second night after leaving the vessel we anchored in the southern part of Peards Bay, our reckoning at noon being 71° 9′ N Lat, Mer Alt, and 159° 27′ Long. D.R. The morning as you know was a fog very thick. I did not like to track, the Pinnace and second whaler being to windward and out of sight; although not far off, feared I might lose them or should have been closer in shore. Neither of them heard my musket signals. We lay at this anchorage only two hours to get wood. Between it and Cape Smythe every place likely to afford shelter has been looked into without success, not even Refuge Inlet. I sounded it on Saturday night and on the bar got only 3 feet, and that so narrow that I consider it entirely out of the question as a place for the boats. I shall not take the larger boats further on than we now are. Hope to leave tomorrow as there is now a strong NE wind, also a current of two knots through the channel setting SW with large floes of drift ice. Standing up for the ice yesterday it appeared quite connected with the land, when I stood to the Westward along the pack hoping there was a passage there. I saw the *Nancy Dawson* running towards us at 6. I boarded her when Mr Shedden informed me of his having been up to 72° N, was then stopped by the pack and ran it, down to this point. He anchored about an hour after us 1/8 of a mile south of the Western of the two ice bergs we were lying between. This morning heavy masses of field ice about us, and the channel completely blocked up, with a strong NE wind. The *Owen* schooner, had to haul close under the lee of an ice berg in consequence, the Pinnace doing so last evening to get clear of the drift. Under these circumstances, I do not consider it prudent to start. I shall therefore hold on till the Channel is clear, and wind moderate.

We have had beautiful weather, and a very clear sea until Saturday night. In fact up to that time we had seen more ice off Wainwright Inlet and the "Sea Horse Islands". We have had a great many natives with whom I have rubbed noses. They have been very friendly, but today when the boats were lying under the berg, preparing for the start, they suddenly decamped, and on overhauling missed one of the boats crutches, Mr Shedden's, and two gangway brasses for side ropes. Our boats are certainly very deep, as I am most anxious to take as much provision as possible, that we may not distress Fort Good Hope in the event of our reaching it, or any other of the Hudson's Bay Companys' Establishments, as I do not think it likely I shall get back again this season. I have loaded them up with 70 days from this time, including Mr Hooper, Mate, and myself. I intend to leave Mr Martin, 2nd Master, with the larger boats, thinking him better adapted for the Service, and not knowing how to use the Foxe's dipping instrument. I did say in the former part of this letter I should not take the larger boats further on, but seeing the whalers so deep, I shall not part with them till I get to Point Barrow, then return to the edge of the pack.

The natives as far as we can understand like ships. The interpreter had not understood them well, although he had made himself generally useful. On overhauling the bread I find we are nearly 300 pounds short, without counting the two sacks I left behind. As Mr Shedden has appeared to let us have whatever we want, I have filled up and have directed Mr. Martin to get a supply from him when he required it. I also found wanting a pick axe and a shovel, with which he has supplied me. In fact his attention and willingness to assist in every possible way has been quite beyond my praise, nor have I any means of making adequate return. I shall leave to you, Sir, to do what is right on this occasion. I have got the latitude and longitude together with a few extracts from his log which may be perhaps interesting.

And now Sir, I must bring this to a conclusion as I think I have given you all particulars. I need hardly say, how anxious I am, as well as my men, to get on, but it would be madness to start with such a breeze blowing and the boats so deep. I am happy to say all are well, and the men have conducted themselves much to my satisfaction. For our success I cannot say. I hope we all know with whom that rests, and trust He will be pleased to grant it as particularly by finding those of whom we are in search, and remove all danger and difficulty from our path. With kind remembrance Captain Kellett, all my messmates and shipmates in the *Herald*, not forgetting those in the *Plover*.

> I remain with every respect,
> Yours faithfully,
> (Sgd) W.J.S. Pullen.
> Lieut. H.B.M.S. *Plover*.[6]

Lieutenant Pullen sent a second report of proceedings and a private letter, both addressed to Captain Kellett, by hand of Mr. Martin, Second Master, when he parted company with the expedition on the night of 4 August about forty miles east-south-east of Point Barrow.

Pullen's second report of proceedings reads:

> Schooner *Owen*, north of a low
> sandy islet, extending nearly
> east and west in 1 fm sandy
> bottom. Lat 71° 12′ N, 154° 56′ W

> 4 August 1849.

Sir,

I beg leave to forward by return of the decked boats a copy of my proceedings up to this time. We anchored here yesterday afternoon just as a heavy breeze from the SSW was coming on, accompanied with rain, and immediately commenced stowing the whale boats and a baidar[7], which I bought from the natives at Point Barrow. We left the place from which my last was dated, on the evening of the 31st July, making good progress. From the open sea in the Channel leading North between the packed ice and the main, hoped to reach Point Barrow that night. The wind was NE and a strong Southerly [going] tide against us. At 11 to our disappointment, we were most effectually stopped, miles from the point. The ice from the land to the main pack formed in one solid body, some of it aground in 4 fm water. All we could do now was to wait patiently for a change in the wind. The next day, the 1st of August, wind still the same and occasionally a thick fog. We managed to get on about a mile by tracking, and secured to the shore ice in latitude 71° 20′ 30″ N. With the Ice Master I pulled alongside with one of the whale boats, the whole edge of the grounded ice up to the main pack, without discovering any passage or chance of one. I decided that if tomorrow did not see the edge of the ice clear, to head the two boats over the narrow part of the land of Point Barrow, and push through by Elsons Bay, as the sea was there clear. In the evening I landed and visited the natives, who mustered very strong, but were very friendly and glad to see us. I went to their tents, in fact all over their camp. When they all assembled, I shall say no less than 80 men, women and children, for an hour they danced for our amusement. I gave them a few beads, tobacco, snuff, and returned to the vessel accompanied by a few. One of them having been wounded in the hand requested me to dress it. I did so, as well as possible, and sent him away with a cleaner hand than I think he had ever had before. I had not been half an hour on board when I heard a heavy gun to the Southward. I thought it might be the *Plover*, and pulled away in the direction with the fog so thick I was not able to see. I soon saw the *Nancy Dawson* who seems determined to go as far as possible. In the night about eleven o'clock the wind veered to SE and South. By 4 o'clock the ground ice was on the move, driving to the Northward with a current of at least 2 knots.

At 5 we were off, and at 7 came to in 2 fms water, one hundred fathoms off shore of Point Barrow. Here I landed to erect a mark, and get sights, and look for the post Elson left. I could not find it, therefore went on with our observations. The dip 82.4°, the latitude, longitude and variation, I have not worked, leaving it for a future time when I have more to spare. I send you by Mr Martin the observations.

At Point Barrow we were on shore all day, and were well received by the natives who constantly surrounded us, but no trouble. They were quiet and orderly which we particularly wanted while getting our observations.

I can assure you it gives me great pleasure being able to speak of them in this way. I bought a baidar for the purpose of taking all our provisions. The whale boats are floating very deep with even only 50 days. We do not (may not) come back, as I confidently hope to reach the Mackenzie from the open and clear sea now around us.

We anchored in this spot yesterday afternoon, just as a stiff breeze was coming in from SSW. We went on with our loading and start today, sending Mr Martin and the two large boats back. I have given him only three weeks provisions, taking all his remainder myself to guard against no supply at Fort Hope, if we are obliged to seek it. Mr Shedden has followed us up most perseveringly. Now I have every reason to think he is at Point Barrow, as he was under weigh yesterday morning, driving with the ice which surrounded him to the North. He will let Mr Martin have provisions if required, and bury a quantity at Refuge Inlet. The mark I left at Point Barrow was 20 feet in length, with a cross in it, and painted (on it) was "*Plovers* boats arrived on the 2nd August — Intelligence 10 feet NE." In a hole (was buried) a preserved meat tin with a letter stating where going, how many men, what provisions, and that the large boats return again, staying as long as possible off the pack, also the places of rendezvous of *Herald* and *Plover*, with ever hope of our success.

> I remain
> Sir
>   Your obedient servant,
>   (Sgd) W.J.S. Pullen, Lieutenant,
>   H.M.B. *Plover*.[8]

Pullen also sent the following private letter to Captain Kellett:

Night of the 4th August, 1849.

My dear Captain Kellett,

I wrote to you from the edge of the Pack, and then thought that we should have been much further in advance than we now are, but ice is terrible to deal with. However I do not despair, and confidentially hope to reach the Mackenzie, but still so late that I do not expect to get back again, I bought a baidar off Point Barrow, that I am not in any way afraid of want should we have to winter at "Fort Hope." I am now just on the start again from our present position, Lat 71° 12′ N, Long 154° 56′ W, with a clear open sea and a fair wind. I stayed at Point Barrow all the 2nd, got the dip, 82.4°, observations for time, latitude and declination, but not worked. The Second Master [Mr Martin] who I send back with the boats has got them and can give you particulars.

The small compass you so kindly lent me I send back, as I did not recollect at the time I had one myself.

Mr Shedden has followed us up quite to Point Barrow. I hope he is now all clear, his kindness has been unbounded, assisting us in every way. It is now quite fair. For the last day we have had strong breezes from South and SSW with heavy rain.

I fear we cannot take the interpreter, he is very ill, and seems to be frightened. I think his room would be better than his company. He has been of little use, in fact does not understand the natives *here*. We have got on with them famously, and have been among them as old standing friends. I will now wind this up as time is now drawing near for our start.

May God bless you Sir for your kindness, and I hope we

shall meet again, with kind remembrances to all on board. Believe me, Sir,

Yours very truly,
(Sgd) W.J.S. Pullen.

P.S. Captain Moore in his orders says if I am obliged to seek Fort Hope, I am to make the best of my way to York Factory, and report myself to the Admiralty. In that case I shall hardly get back next season, but go home with the Hudson's Bay Ships.[9]

Captain Kellett sent copies of Pullen's reports of Proceedings and his private letters to the Admiralty. They were enclosed with his own report which was dated 22 November 1849.[10] This was forwarded from Mazatlan, on the west coast of Mexico, where the *Herald* arrived on 14 November 1849. All this correspondence reached the Admiralty on 22 January 1850, and was published in *The Times* on 24 and 25 January 1850. Nothing more was heard of Pullen and his small party, until his next report was received on 30 April 1850.

When Mr. Martin with the two large boats parted company eastward of Point Barrow, Lieutenant Pullen was faced with a voyage of about five hundred miles along the north coast of Alaska and Canada to the delta of the Mackenzie River, and a further 750 miles up that river to Fort Simpson. He had two twenty-seven-foot gig whale boats and a umiak, all well loaded with provisions and stores for the expedition. His party consisted of fourteen officers and men. To seaward he faced the Polar Pack, the ice of the Beaufort Sea, while along the coast the water was shallow and relatively unknown. Apart from a few Eskimo camps, there was no settlement until he reached Fort McPherson, and that was about a hundred miles up the Peel River, a tributary of the Mackenzie. When the moment came to start on this hazardous voyage, Pullen must have wondered at his chances of success, for it was not only a great challenge, but a dangerous undertaking. Fourteen men and three small, open boats against the Arctic sea and the grim, inhospitable wilderness of northern Canada. It says much for the courage, seamanship and resolution of this small party that they were prepared to face such hardship in the search for Sir John Franklin and his expedition.

The boat expedition set off on the night of 4 August, and by the 13th had reached Return Reef, which was Franklin's farthest point west in his voyage along the coast in 1826. It was here that Pullen had trouble with the Eskimos, who were very aggressive and finally fired two arrows at the party. Pullen and Hooper returned the fire and, although no one was hit, this had the desired effect of discouraging any further action. On 17 August the party camped for the night on Barter Island. This was the place where a man called Spence, one of the boats' crew of the Franklin-Back expedition of 1825-26, had left a musket and some ammunition on the beach.[11] The musket and a powder horn were seen by Pullen in the possession of an Eskimo at Return Reef.

On the evening of 21 August, the party took shelter under the lee of Herschel Island, and six days later they entered the delta of the Mackenzie River. Here they camped while Lieutenant Pullen, with Mr. Abernethy, the Ice Master, and six men set off to visit Whale Island, as directed by Commander Moore in his instructions to Lieutenant Pullen. They got as far as Ellice Island before they were stopped by a north-westerly gale. This, together with a mixture of rain, sleet, hail and snow, forced them to give up the attempt and return to the camp. After mistaking the Rat River for the Peel, Pullen and his party eventually reached Fort McPherson on 5 September. Here he left Mr. Hooper, with five men and one boat, for the winter. Some of the men were suffering from exhaustion and were in no state to face the long struggle up the Mackenzie. Pullen and seven men left the fort on 6 September, taking with them one of the Hudson's

Bay Company men as a guide. At Point Separation he found a message from Sir John Richardson dated 31 July 1848, telling him to make for Fort Simpson. By 11 September it became obvious that they could not handle both a gig whale boat and the umiak as they tracked up the river. The umiak was broken up and the skins were saved for moccasins. On the evening of 14 September the party reached Fort Good Hope where they were supplied with moccasins to replace their heavy leather sea boots, which were most unsuitable for tracking. Here the whale boat and practically all their stores were left. A Company boat, probably a York Boat, was provided, together with four men to help in getting her and Pullen's weary men safely to Fort Simpson. By the morning of 17 September they were under way once more, and six days later reached Fort Norman. Here they obtained some provisions, discharged two of the Company's men, and set off again, reaching Fort Simpson on 3 October 1849. They were welcomed by Dr. Rae who was in charge of the fort, and who must have been rather astonished at meeting sailors so far from the sea.[12]

The following day Pullen wrote his report of proceedings addressed to the Secretary of the Admiralty, which was received on 30 April 1850. It reads as follows:-

Fort Simpson, Mackenzie River,
October 4th. 1849.

Sir,

I beg to acquaint you for their Lordships information of my arrival at this place yesterday morning with the greater part of my party, having left the remainder with an officer, Mr Hooper, Acting Mate, at one of the Hudson's Bay Posts on the River Peel. I left the *Plover* off Wainwright Inlet on the night of the 25th of July 1849, in pursuance of orders from Commander Moore, a copy of which I herewith send, together with those of Captain Kellett of H.M. Ship *Herald*. Our voyage has been successful with the exception and

main object of not finding any traces of our missing and
unfortunate countrymen. Extracts from my journal of proceedings I can only at this time send as an extra express will
be sent directly the boats arrive from the Great Slave Lake,
momentarily expected, and where the party pass the winter; and it will only be by great exertion that the express
will save the open water. A track chart and complete journal I hope to lay before their Lordships on my arrival in
England, leaving this for York Factory about the middle of
June 1850, and expect to arrive there the latter end of
August.

On the night of the 25th of July 1849 off Wainwright
Inlet, H.M. Brig *Plover*, H.M. Ship *Herald* and Schooner Yacht
Nancy Dawson in company, I shoved off from the first named
vessel (receiving three hearty cheers), the same from the
Herald on passing her, which we about to prosecute the
search for gallant Sir J. Franklin and his party, heartily
returned, with four boats viz, the *Herald*'s decked boat
called the *Owen*, the *Plover*'s pinnace and two whale boats,
with a crew of five and twenty including Officers and
myself; seventy days provisions for each man and twenty
cases of Pemmican. On Sunday the 29th early in the morning passed Cape Smyth and soon after came up with the
main pack of ice, close into the shore and stretching westward as far as the eye could reach. I now thought our voy-
aging was over, and we should have to return to our ship.
The wind was NE, so I hauled to the westward and ran
along the pack in hopes of finding a passage there. At one
time I fancied I saw an opening when I saw the *Nancy
Dawson* coming towards us. She is commanded and owned
by a Mr. Shedden, formerly a mate in our Service, and
from whom I received very valuable assistance and great
kindness. He seemed determined to keep by us, following as
long and as far as possible. At noon I got the latitude on the
ice, 71° 15′ 58″ N, and on looking well round I saw a narrow lane of open water close in shore leading to the north-

ward, but apparently blocked up at its entrance. I made for the shore again when we were visited by natives, who gave us to understand there was a narrow passage close in shore leading up the coast. Here our interpreter was at fault. He could not talk to these people or make himself understood a bit better than we could; gaining all our information by signs succeeding to admiration, the Esquimaux being apparently so used to that mode of receiving and imparting information. As we got in shore we saw the Channel in the bottom and nearly centre of a deep bay formed by the pack and main land, the western horn being about 2 miles off shore. There was heavy ice driving through it together with a current of 2 knots, and wind dead end on (NNE light). It was impossible to get on, so I anchored in 4½ fms, between two bergs at the mouth of the Bay, to wait for an opportunity of getting through. As the ice was driving fast down on us, I weighed and made fast to the western bay under the lee.

The next morning the yacht took a berth alongside of us, mooring with two ice anchors. During the night of the 30th as well as all day it blew hard from NNE. On the morning of the 31st not quite so much wind, but still heavy ice driving down the channel. Our friendly berg parted and set all adrift, surrounded by heavy floes and drift ice. The boats were soon again fast under the lee of the inshore or Eastern Bay, where the *Dawson* again took up her berth, working up and threading her way through the high ice and against a strong current in gallant style. Toward evening the wind began to moderate. At 6.30 pm sent the two whale boats to pull close in shore, while the large ones turned up with a moderate breeze until 9 pm when it had hauled so much to the westward that we stood along the shore and took our small craft in tow. As we advanced we saw many natives who tried every inducement to get us to land, dancing and shouting. They followed us till we came to the southern part of the low narrow spit terminating to the northward in

47

Point Barrow, which we were in hopes of reaching by twelve o'clock. We were disappointed, for at 11 pm we were stopped by an immense floe effectually blocking up the channel, so we hauled close into the shore under a projecting point of ice lying on the beach and secured. Here we were visited by many natives, quite friendly and apparently delighted to see us, offering their furs for trifling pieces of tobacco and helping us in various ways. It was light all night, but rather cold, the thermometer standing at 33°.

The next morning the ice had driven off shore a little and allowed us to get on, partly under sail and partly tracking, in which the natives readily took a share. At 11 am. we were effectually stopped; the ice from the shore to the main pack quite fast and no channel as far as the eye could reach. Hauled close in under the lee of a projecting point from the beach and made fast. The wind was moderate from NE, off shore, so it might clear a passage for us; but no, it was too heavy, altho much of it is shore ice from its colour. Our latitude at noon was 71° 20′ 30″ N. In the afternoon hauled close up to the ice and tried to force a passage, but it was useless. Many parts of it were aground in 5 fms water but went away fast. In the evening I landed amongst the natives, and was most graciously received by rubbing noses; they dancing and shouting to each other with stentorian lungs, and shewing us round their camps with evident satisfaction. At one in particular, the chief apparently, assembled his people and entertained us for an hour with dancing, accompanied with singing and music on a sort of tambourine, a thin skin (intestine of the seal) well stretched on a circular frame of wood, and beat against a stick. I gave them beads, tobacco and snuff, winding up with a scramble at which they were as much pleased as our men. It was a ridiculous sight, so many (women and all) wrapped up in furs, rolling on the ground together. We parted good friends, many following us to the boat, where I dressed the hand of one man who had received a wound in it while seal hunting. I'm sure it never had such a washing before as I gave it.

At 11 this night the wind hauled to the SE, and shortly after the ice began to break. I heard the booming of a heavy gun, which I returned with a small three pounder we had in the bows of the *Owen*, and then pulled down the coast in hopes of seeing the *Plover*. It was foggy at the time, but on its breaking away a little I discovered the *Nancy Dawson* most perseveringly following us up. I went on board and tried to persuade Mr. Shedden to return south as his vessel was quite unfit to encounter the ice, but no. He was determined to follow us as far as he possibly could with a chance of getting back. At 12 the ice was driving northward. A large floe coming up from the south drove the schooner which was at anchor, close in shore, but not on the ground, as it was checked by projecting points from the beach. As she was not in any danger I left her, returning to my boats with a current setting to the northward at the rate of 1½ knots an hour. At 5.30 am, seeing our obstruction in full move, we made sail after it, threading our way through the loose pieces towards Point Barrow. At 7 rounded it and came to in 2 fms water, one hundred feet off shore, with unmingled feelings of delight, and silent thanks of gratitude to that merciful Providence who had conducted us thus far in safety, and with a prayer for a continuation of His help on our voyage. I now had to consider and determine on my future proceedings. It did not take me long; for with a fine open sea to the eastward, I concluded there would be little difficulty in reaching the Mackenzie, and resolved to make a bold push. I landed among a large concourse of natives, recognizing many of our former friends. Got observations for time, dip and variation; [Point Barrow 71° 23′ 22″ N, 156° 28′ 30″ W.], set up a large pole with directions on it for finding buried information of our movements, and that there were two ships in the Arctic Seas; one to winter at Kotzebue or Fort Clarence. Purchased a baidar and gave

49

the natives a few trinkets and tobacco with which they were highly delighted. At 11 o'clock that night we were all ready for a move, while the yacht, a mile south of the point, was driving up with the ice. Shortly after, Mr. Shedden came on board, having walked up the coast after landing two miles below to see the last of us. His boat came soon after, and we got under weigh at half past 11 of the night of the 2nd of August, parting with mutual good wishes for success. I hope and trust he got clear and away to the southward without any difficulty.

We made sail to the eastward with a light northerly air and easterly set, threading our way through loose ice until 2 o'clock, afternoon of the 3rd, when we anchored in 5 feet water two hundred feet from the shore off a low sandy spit, in Latitude 71° 15′ N, and Longitude 155° 37′ W. It was now blowing hard from the south, and kept us here until the night of the 4th when the weather moderated. Our three boats were loaded, and were named, the first whaler *Louisa*, the second *Logan*, and the baidar *Supply*. I gave Mr. Martin directions to return to Refuge Inlet with the large boats, and there wait as long as he considered it prudent. He was on no account to run the risk of being caught by the ice, or north of Icy Cape after the first week of September. On the first indication of it he was to get away to the southward and rejoin the ship, finding her at either of the places mentioned in Commander Moore's orders. Refuge Inlet we examined coming up the coast, but found it not available for large boats. My crew consisted of eleven men, three of them petty officers, John Abernethy, Acting Second Master Ice, Mr. Hooper, Acting Mate and myself, fourteen in number.[13]

In my orders I was directed to take Mr. Martin, but as Mr. Hooper was the magnetic observer I made the change, particularly as Commander Moore had left it entirely to myself on speaking to him about it. The interpreter also I did not bring on, as up to Point Barrow I found him useless.

He did not understand the natives, in fact none of the northern tribes, and told us so shortly after starting. Again, when I was first going to leave this night I found him very ill. I waited for an hour but no improvement, so I resolved not to delay any longer, and lose the light wind which was now blowing from the south. At 11.45 pm, shoved off with three hearty cheers from those we left behind us, and who would most gladly have come on to share our danger and our difficulty. Mr. Martin in particular was much cut up, and greatly disappointed at not taking the large boats further on, but I did not like to run the risk. I considered now we had fully ninety days provisions, besides twenty cases of pemmican. Our little craft were certainly very deep; but we had light hearts and every hope of success in reaching our destination. We kept close in shore with the wind from SSW, a moderate breeze.[14]

During the afternoon of 24 August, H.M.S. *Herald* was in the vicinity of Point Hope, about forty miles SSW of Cape Lisburne. The *Owen* and the *Nancy Dawson* were sighted in shore, and in due course Mr. Martin and Mr. Shedden arrived on board the *Herald*. Mr. Martin then delivered to Captain Kellett the private letter and the report of proceedings which Lieutenant Pullen had given to him when they parted company east of Point Barrow. Both were dated 4 August 1849.

Captain Kellett in his report to the Admiralty, dated 22 November 1849, said:

I have sent their Lordships copies of Mr. Pullen's letters, both public and private, that have been received since his departure. From them they will gain more information than I could afford.

Through these letters their Lordships will also see with what a noble and proper spirit Lieutenant Pullen undertook his voyage, being nevertheless fully alive to its dangers and exposure.

I am quite sure their Lordships when they appointed Mr. Pullen, were fully aware of his character and capabilities. I trust, however, that they will not consider the following comments out of place: —

I don't know any officer more capable of conducting with success such an expedition. He possesses health, great bodily strength, and endurance, ability, and great decision of character. Coupled with all these good points in their leader, the boats had an open sea and a fair wind, so that I have no apprehensions as to their reaching one of the Hudson's Bay's establishments on the Mackenzie early in this season, though not sufficiently early to return to Kotzebue Sound this year.

Dease and Simpson certainly made their voyage from the Mackenzie to Point Barrow and back in one season, but they travelled west, at the commencement of the season, and returned to the eastward at its close, when the winds prevailed from the westward. Our boats would have to return to the westward at the latter part of the season, which I believe to be impossible from the packing of the ice, the heavy westerly winds and currents. Mr. Pullen's letter says pretty plainly that he will not return; he will therefore be waiting their Lordship's instructions at York Factory.[15]

The account of the boat expedition goes on:

At 11.30 am [5 August] passed Point Christie, crossed Dease Inlet and at 2.50 pm landed on a low point in Fatigue Bay for dinner. As the wind was blowing fresh, altho favourable, I remained here til 5 pm, for our heavily laden boats were in no condition to stand heavy seas. By that time it was a little more moderate, so we shoved off, passed Boat Extreme, Cape Governor Simpson and were getting well across Smith's Bay. With an increasing breeze, now from the westward, and the sea getting up, we tried to keep closer to shore, but the water was so shoal we were obliged to haul off again. At 7 the *Logan* with the *Supply* in tow, made a signal of distress, so I shorten'd sail and pulled toward them. I found the latter shipping a great deal of water from being so deep. Took some stores out of her, and I with the *Louisa* took her in tow. This was almost out of the frying pan into the fire, as the extra weight in the whalers rendered their situation ticklish; but there was no help for it, and we all kept close together. At 9 pm we were obliged to land on a dead lee shore with the sea breaking right over us, in the eastern part of Smith's Bay. Hauled the boats up and unloaded them. Found all our bread wet, with the exception of 120 lbs in a cask, and almost 100 lbs of flour. The preserved potatoes were saturated, with all our small stock of clothing in a like condition. We camped in a low boggy situation, but the best we could find, and made the most of it.

The next morning, the 6th, still blowing and raining. We built a sort of oven and commenced drying our bread which kept us at work all day and the watch all night. It was then only imperfectly done, for it took more time than I was willing to spare, particularly as in the evening the wind was falling and the sea going down. Since leaving the large boats we have not seen much ice, and now to the north as far as the eye can reach is a clear open sea. Crossing Smith's Bay we could see the Pack from 4 to 5 miles distant.

On the morning of the 7th the weather was almost calm. We launched our boats and loaded them; sorry to find that a great quantity of our bread is still wet, which we are likely to lose, as well as six tins of preserved potatoes. At 11 we shoved off, the *Logan* taking the lead, the *Louisa* (my boat) with *Supply* in tow. We pulled up the eastern shores of the Bay close to, rounded Point Drew and landed a few miles east of it. We got our dinners, and the dip, and at 3 moved on again, winding our way among drift ice, with the wind light from the eastward. At 8.30 we landed for the night by the deer pond and salt creek of Simpson, with the wind from SE.

The morning of the 8th was fine with a light haze and moderate wind from SE. At 5.30 we shoved off, and on the morning of the 9th at five minutes after 8 am, landed on the SE part of Cape Halket, and got the dip. It was now perfectly calm, and cloudy sky with the pack from two to three miles off shore. At a quarter to 10 we shoved off under oars and steered a course for Point Berens, the eastern horn of Harrison's Bay. I found the current setting eastward, a great help to us. At 11 am we entered the ice (right in our way), the sea being covered with large floes as far as the eye could reach, and some aground in 5 fms water. At 4.30 pm a heavy squall of rain with wind from SW, to which we made sail, and hauled a little to the southward to close the land, the sky looking very threatening. Quantities of drift wood passing, driving to the northward as well as the ice.

On the morning of the 10th the breeze began to increase, and the sea get up, and our poor little vessels to labor very much, shipping water and keeping our bailers constantly going. At 2 am our soundings had been gradually decreasing from 3½ to 1 fm, and we were all looking anxiously for land, to get ashore as soon as possible. The *Logan* had the *Supply* in tow, when at 2.30 am she parted her tow rope, but secured her again. At 3 sighted land, very low, which I take to be about the mouth of the Colville, from the shallow water and large quantities of drift wood. At 3.15 am the water had shoaled to 2 feet and before we could haul off were aground. We poled into deep water and stood to the northward. At 3.30 am a strong breeze and heavy sea with the land barely in sight. I found it absolutely necessary to make for it, a dead lee shore as it was, and offered a landing at all risk, the wind being about west. At one time I was doubtful whether the *Supply* would reach it, the *Louisa* and *Logan* being very little better. At 3.40 am the *Supply* pitched under, and with the weight of water broke off her head rails and tore the skin adrift. This was soon laced up again. It was now necessary to lighten if we were to get on shore; so I gave the word and we threw overboard some of our lading, confining ourselves to that damaged in the last gale. Our boats felt the relief directly, and at 6.30 am we reached the shore, landing pretty well about two miles south of Point Berens, with the exception of all hands getting an addition to our already wet garments. Cleared and hauled the boats up, and on overhauling found we had thrown overboard 250 lbs of bread, seven cases of preserved potatoes and a ten gallon cask of water, making it most imperative on us to be very careful on what we have got. I now consider the worst part of our voyage over, no more deep bays to cross, but able to keep the land close on board.

On the morning of the 11th we were again all ready to proceed with dry clothes and cheerful hearts, and at 7.30 am shoved off. We pulled up for Point Berens, and at ten minutes to 9 am landed, as I intended burying some pemmican which would be a relief to our boats, and on a conspicious point likely to be visited by those we are in search of, if successful, in getting down to these shores proceeding to the westward. We met here a great many natives, all friendly and glad to see us, to whom I made presents, and made our cache without their observing it. The direction post we could not hide, but let it very deep into the soil. On shoving off we missed our shovel. One of the men observed a native burying something in the sand and stand on it. I walked up to him, fully expecting it was the missing article, and on trying to find out what it was, he resisted. Mr. Hooper pushed his hand completely through the sand, got hold of the shovel and hauled it from under him. The fellow was disappointed and followed us to the boat, and while shoving off made another attempt to get it, with no better success. We ran to the eastward with the wind from WNW, between Jone's Isle and the main. At 2.15 pm landed for dinner, and were soon joined by a baidar or omiak full of men and one woman, among whom we recognized our friend who had attempted to steal the shovel. We did not allow them to come beyond a certain boundary line. At 2.30 pm we started again with the wind from NW, still following the shore as close as the shoal water would permit. When we were abreast of the western part of Return Reef we crossed over to it and ran along its southern shores. While crossing over we observed the omiak following us, but keeping a respectable distance. At 8.30 pm we landed on the Return Reef and were soon visited by a party of natives who were quite friendly. I gave them a few beads and small pieces of tobacco. One of them, apparently a chief, was very desirous of getting powder. He had a musket of English manufacture, Barnet the name on it, also a powder horn with about a quarter of a lb. of powder in it, but no shot.[16]

At 11.30 pm we shoved off again and saw approaching us four omiaks full of men and a few women, and observed two large camps, one on the point of the main abreast of us, the other and larger, on a point a little to the eastward of it. We were now pulling to the eastward with ever appearance of a freshening breeze from NE, and five large omiaks keeping close up with us. In one I counted twenty-three, two out of the number women, and none of the others less than sixteen. We kept close order, not allowing them to approach too near.

On passing the large camp they tried hard to induce us to land, without success, so they left us, and as I thought for good. At 2.15 am of the 12th we were under the necessity of pulling in for the shore. We landed on a very shallow beach about half a mile westward of Point Beechy, after making but little progress against a strong North Easterly wind, and the sea getting up. At 3 am the natives came up to us again, walking along the shore from their camp about two miles off, having certainly watched us all the time. They now mustered in large numbers; there could not be less than eighty, among whom I recognized our friend of Point Berens who tried to steal our shovel, and the chief with his musket, carried by his wife, and several other women present besides. I felt no apprehension, but at the same time had all ready to embark at a moment's notice. I drew a line for their boundary, and saw them all seated on their proper side. The man with the musket crossed over and made many demands for powder, which I would not give him and motioned him off. On seeing me resolute in refusing, he gave the gun to his wife, walked a short distance to their camp and returned almost immediately with his bow and arrows, the whole of the men doing the same. I gave the word to get into the boats, but to do it leisurely and show them we were ready. Mr. Hooper, the two marines and self kept a sharp lookout with musket in hand. I ordered the *Logan* and *Supply* to shove off and get into deep water. In the meantime this chief tried hard to get on the bank and to windward of us, but I would not allow him. When the remainder of us made a move to the *Louisa*, they made a rush for the bank, and I expect, hoped to catch us now at a disadvantage, but we were all in the boat, Mr. Hooper and I with our double barrels at the present, while the other men were shoving off and pulling out to the *Logan*. One fellow had the arrow on the string and bow at full stretch. Fortunately I covered him and he dropped down under the bank immediately. We lost our anchors, otherwise everything was all right.

As the wind was too strong to proceed eastward, I ran back to that part of the Return Reef we had previously landed on. As the *Supply* was nearly full of water, I took out of her three cases of pemmican and buried it in the sand. Before I could get marks up, the natives were after us again, having landed half a mile on the reef to the eastward of us, just as we were shoving off. I now made an attempt to pull up for the pack; distant about two miles from the northern part of the reef, with quantities of drift ice close down on the northern shore. We passed through an opening in the reef, all strung on together to keep close, with two large omiaks full of men, about forty, following and ranging up alongside occasionally. They kept at a respectable distance, apparently watching for an opportunity for attack, which I really think they would have tried if for one moment they had seen our eyes off them. We pulled for an hour without making any advance against a heavy sea and strong breeze, and tiring the men to no purpose. I bore up again for the reef and landed on its weather shore. We hauled our boats up immediately and built a stockade of the drift timber, quantities of which were near at hand. We got all ready for resisting any attack they might make, having landed half a mile to the eastward of us. At the same time a large party did the same to the westward, mustering in all about one hundred men. Three men tried to approach us, but I would not allow it, keeping an armed watch just on the site of the reef, which they seeing did not trouble us any more that day, but watched us. At 10 am they left us, returning to the main land.

It was impossible for us to move with the present weather, blowing hard from NE, with a heavy sea and the ice driving fast down on the reef, and immense masses assuming all sorts of appearances. On one occasion this afternoon the men came running to me and shouting "a Sail, Sir, there is the Schooner." I looked, and it certainly did look like a vessel, but on examining with the glass I saw directly it was a large berg in the pack. The night before I was deceived in nearly the same way. Passing between the main and Jones's Island under sail, directly we opened the passage between it and the western part of Return Reef and got sight of the ice, I made certain there was a boat coming down towards us. So sure was I that we down sail and pulled dead to the windward for a long way. On near approach we saw it was only ice. In the evening Mr. Hooper visited the spot where we had buried the pemmican and found it untouched.

The morning of the 13th was cold and rainy with the wind fresh from the north, and very hazy weather which I determined to take advantage of and get away from our troublesome friends. At 2 am we shoved off, leaving a large fire inside our stockade, and pulled directly for the pack. At 4 am made fast to a large berg close to it, and commenced preparing our breakfast (boiling our kettle with spirits of wine), which we got shivering with the cold and almost dripping wet with sea water and damp fog. At 8.15 we shoved off from our cold berth and pulled away to the eastward following close along the pack, and passing between large bergs with a NE wind and the current setting westward. At 10 am to our inexpressable joy the wind hauked to the westward, made all sail, and at half past twelve landed on the eastern part of Return Reef, about two miles from its extreme point. Large fires soon dried our wet clothes and got us a warmer dinner, fitting us again for anything. As we were getting our things into the boats, we saw two omiaks coming out from under the land, paddle up and land to the westward of us just as we were shoving off, and quite bent on doing us mischief if they could. Every man, forty in number, had his bow and arrows, and directly, as they thought within distance, fired two arrows, one dropping astern and one ahead. Mr. Hooper and I fired over them, which they returned. We then fired amongst them, but I am happy to say without effect, as just then both parties were out of range, and we saw our balls skip along towards them. Nevertheless it made them drop flat on the ground, and they were evidently frightened. We now made sail and resumed our course with a fine breeze from the WNW. At half past twelve at night we landed on a low shingly point two miles to the eastward of Foggy Island, tired and weary after two days of excitement and continued watching. We were wet through the greatest part of the time, with the thermometer from 35° to 40°, considering the latter quite warm. Since leaving the Return Reef we had not seen any ice.

The next morning until 8 o'clock we passed the Lion and Reliance Reefs; and on the morning of the 16th landed on the eastern part of Flaxman's Island, with the pack about a mile from its seaward shore, but the drift close down. We passed between the island and the main in a free channel. At 1.15 pm we landed on the low sandy beach from the high eastern part of the island. The ice apparently close down, but on getting on this high part, a passage along the shore was distinctly seen, as well as in Camden Bay. At 2.15 pm we were again moving, threading our way through the ice, occasionally tracking where the shoal water allowed us to land. The wind was light from the eastward; the main pack from two to three miles off shore, with a great quantity of sailing ice about. At 10 we made fast for the night to a small grounded berg. We were not able to get on shore as the water was so shoal, so we slept in our boats. Night was now throwing her sable mantle over us which we all seemed to welcome as an old acquaintance, having for nearly the last two months daylight throughout the twenty-four hours.

The next morning at 4 am we found the ice had driven off shore; perfectly calm and smooth water; cast off and pulling eastward. We landed at 5 to get our breakfast on a small spit where there was an immense tree amongst the drift timber, perfectly straight, 80 feet in length, and 10 feet in circumference at its base. From 6.30 am up to noon the ice was very thick, when we got into fine open water and made good progress with a light WSW wind, which sprang up just as we got clear, it appearing to have been shut out before by the ice. The main pack was distant about four miles off shore, with very little drift ice visible. At 1 passed a very large camp, but no natives were seen. At 9.15 landed on the SW part of Barter Island and camped for the night.

The next morning, 18th, we started with the wind from north-east. At 11.30 am we landed on the northern part of a small island eastward of Manning Point, and got a meridian altitude and the dip. Here I buried cases of pemmican and erected a post with directions on it for finding it. At 8 pm we again stopped for the night on a small spit off Point Martin, having made but little progress, the wind against us all day, and strong.

The next day we were detained with a north-east gale and thick fog, the thermometer during the day from 35° to 37°. Fifteen minutes after midnight of the 19th the fog began to clear and the wind shifted to the sw. Our boats which had been lying on the south side of the spit, formerly the lee, now the weather, were shifted round to the northern side and loaded. At 1.15 am of the 20th we shoved off under low sail sometimes driving, as it was dark, and fog not cleared entirely. At 2 am it was broad daylight and we made all sail.

On the evening of the 21st at 7.30 pm we landed for the night on a low shingly beach from one of the islands between Herschel Island and the main, forming for our boats a good lee, the wind then blowing strong from the NW with a heavy sea. The ice here is heavier then any we have yet seen, lying close up to the NW shores of Herschel Island, fast aground, with large floes and sailing ice going fast to the eastward. We were now drawing close to the mouth of the Mackenzie, which I fully hoped to reach in two days at the furtherest; but misfortune still awaited us to the last.

At half-past one on the morning of the 22nd, I was awoke with the disastrous news of all the boats being swamped. On going to them I found it was really so, being occasioned by a sudden shift of wind to sw and breaking their quarter-fasts. We cleared them immediately, and found our instruments the greatest sufferers. The bread we had was already saturated and could receive but little or no additional injury. We turned to with a will, carefully wiped and cleaned all; but I fear the dip circle is injured more than we can remedy, together with my own sextant. However at 8 am we were all ready again, and although we have had such frequent occurrences, no one seemed discouraged. Like sailors, danger and difficulties over, nothing more was thought of it, and no despairing. We were anxious to get on, fearing the ice might block us in where we were now lying, as it was driving fast eastward with the strong north-wester, although a heavy sea on. At 8.30 am we shoved off under close reefs. At eleven we were obliged to seek shelter under the lee of the narrow tongue from the western point of Herschel Island, which forms with the opposite point on the island a deep bay. Here we got our dinners, after which finding both wind and sea gone down, I pushed on, going fast to the eastward with the sailing ice, and under all sail. The *Supply* was doing better alone, but keeping between the *Louisa* and *Logan*. On getting clear of Herschel Island we began to feel the heavy rolling sea, but with no ice in sight. We were again driven to the shore, landing with a good drenching under the lee of a gravel spit, south-east of Catton Point. On these spots we never find water, so we are obliged to carry it with us. Immense quantities of wood is always to be had, and our greatest enjoyment and most comfortable time is sitting or standing before immense fires made of this drift. To-day we took advantage of it as we could not start. We got all things out of the boats, made one long range of fires and spread our bread, now quite a paste, and our drenched garments before it. The spit was of no great size, you might walk round it in five minutes, and just enough elevated in the centre to have our tents and fires in a dry berth. To us it was 'any port in a storm'. I got the dip here. Towards evening the wind was lulling and the sea going down, the sky clearing and stars showing, so we may hope for fine weather to-morrow. Thermometer during the day 35° to 38°.

On the morning of the 23rd it was fine, with a moderate westerly breeze. At ten minutes after 3 am we shoved off and ran away eastward, making good progress. At 3.30 pm we rounded Kay's Point with the wind light, and by 4 quite calm. We did not reach the mouth of the river until the evening of the 26th, passing between Cape Reef and the main where we saw the last of the Esquimaux.

On the evening of the 27th we entered the river, having been employed all day observing and exploring our locality. I was doubtful of my position, but perfectly satisfied of my being on a branch of the Mackenzie. We did not go far up, for Whale Island is yet to be visited.[17] I determined to leave the greater part of the party and Mr. Hooper here on the left bank two miles from its mouth. I proceeded the next day with one boat and seven men including the Ice Master, with a week's provisions; most thankful to that blest Providence who has conducted us thus far in safety.

On the morning of the 28th I left the camp with the wind strong from SW. We ran across Shoal Water Bay and along the north shores of Tent Island, and steered to the NE. In the evening we got up to Ellice Island where we were stopped by strong NW winds and every appearance of a change for the worse, for it was now very cold. During the night it rained hard and blew heavy, clearing up a little in the morning, but with the wind still the same, dead against us, I made up my mind to return. By seven o'clock there was no appearance of change for the better so we shoved off on our way back. We had not made much progress when it came on heavy sleet, followed by hail and finally snow. The piercing cold continued all day with but slight intermission; and I can safely say it has been the most miserable day I have had since the commencement of our voyage. At one time it was so thick and blowing strong that we could only just see the bank we were close to, under which we stopped for such shelter as it afforded, stamping our feet and beating our hands to get them at all warm. There was no walking, the dwarf willow was too thick to allow of it. At six [29th] we reached the camp and found they were not in a much better condition. [Position of the camp according to Pullen's observations was 68° 48′ 45″ North, 135° 40′ 36″ West, Variation 50° 41′ East.]

On the morning of the 5th September we reached the first of the Hudson's Bay Posts, [Fort McPherson in 67° 27′ N, 134° 53′ W. Pullen's observations were 67° 26′ 15″ N, 134° 40′ 19″ W.] and one of which my orders speak of, namely on the Peel River. Our getting here was quite accidental, having mistaken the Rat River, not in my chart, for the mouth of the Peel, and turning into it instead of keeping on. Again, not seeing mountains on the left, as in my chart, I was not sure, although very doubtful.

The night of the 4th an Indian came to us [one of the Louchoux] and told us the white men were not far off. I determined on going on for the next day at least, until I got sufficient observations for what I wanted. It was about 10 am when we reached the post, and were kindly welcomed by Mr. Hardisty, the gentleman in charge. He gave me such good intelligence of being able to keep a part of our party, that I resolved on leaving five of them [the weakest] and Mr. Hooper here, together with one boat and the greatest part of the provision. I gave him orders to join me in the spring of the year, when the Company's people come on with the returns of the year for shipment for England.

I intend pushing on with the rest of the party (seven men) to Point Separation, and the next post cleared the boats, and had the *Logan* and *Supply* loaded with twenty days provisions for eight men, and seven cases of pemmican. On the afternoon of the 6th, taking one of the Company's men as pilot, we shoved off and got to Point Separation the next morning. There I found a note in the "cache" from Sir J. Richardson, saying we were to go to Fort Simpson and winter on the Great Slave Lake.[18] I left three cases of pemmican, nearly equal in weight to one of his, a note with an account of our proceedings, and shoved off, crossed to the right bank and commenced tracking, [the men wearing heavy sea-boots].

By the morning of the 11th I found it very necessary to get rid of one of our boats, namely the *Supply*. Sorry was I to do it, for I had hoped to have carried her to England as a specimen of the Naval architecture of the Western Esquimaux, and for the good service she had rendered us. But there was no help for it, she retarded our progress terribly, and was a great weight to the men in tracking. They were now beginning to feel the work and getting foot-sore and weary, although the strongest of the party. Those I left at Peel River, at least three of them, were in a very weak condition. This was partly my reason, together with Mr. Hardisty's assurance of there being plenty of provision, for leaving them. At all events they have at least fifty day's provision of what we had in the boats, besides four small cases of pemmican. After breaking up the *Supply*, I had the skin cut into three pieces, (considering it would make good mocassins for the men), and stowed it in the *Logan*, together with other stores, which made us very deep, particularly when nine men got into her. She was lighter on the line and we were getting on better. A light breeze sprang up from the south to which we made sail, and on its increasing took all hands in and flew along at a rapid rate, but not daring to keep any distance off shore, so much sea was there raised by the strong wind against the downward current. As our flour and bread were all out, I opened a case of pemmican as a substitute.

On the noon of the 14th we met the Company's boats on their way to the Peel with their winter supply. At 6.30 pm we arrived at Fort Good Hope. [Fort Good Hope in 66° 15′ North, 128° 38′ West. Pullen's observations were 66° 15′ 26″ North, 128° 30′ 12″ West.] Here I remained until Monday morning, getting from Mr. McBeath, the gentleman in charge, a supply of moccasins for the men. The heavy boots [sea-boots] were not at all fit for such work as we have to perform; the walrus hide (skin of *Supply*), made up, also a case of pemmican and quantity of dried meat. We left our boat, the *Logan*, as she is quite unfit for the work, also all the stores we did not require, bringing off nothing but the two marines' muskets. We took one of the Company's boats Mr. McBeath had at the station; two men, a Canadian and a half-breed, the former steersman, and two Indians to assist in tracking; and good service they rendered us, for we should not have been here yet if they had not been with us, not knowing the river, and particularly the rapids, where we should have been at fault.

On Monday the 17th the thermometer at 6 was down to 26°, with a light easterly air. At 7.10 we moved on with the tracking line, and on Sunday the 23rd at noon, we arrived at Fort Norman. [Fort Norman in 64° 54′ N, 125° 34′ W. Pullen's observations were 64° 40′ 18.7″ N, 123° 35′ 50″ W.] Here we got a supply of pemmican, a bag of flour, thirty lbs of dried goats flesh, from Mr. McKenzie, the gentleman in charge. We discharged our two Indians who were as sorry to leave us as we were to part with them, and reached this place [Fort Simpson] on Wednesday, the 3rd October, at 11 o'clock in the forenoon, most hospitably welcomed by Dr. Rae, Mr. Bell and Mr. O'Brien; the former the Arctic voyager, and in charge of the post.[19]

In conclusion, I beg to assure their Lordships that every endeavour has been made to gain intelligence of our missing countrymen; and if I have at all deviated from my orders, it was with a firm conviction that I was doing all for the best. I have had little or no trouble with the natives in making them understand what we wanted; even those with whom we had the skirmish were questioned on our first meeting, and all that we have met, they have looked at us gravely and with astonishment. Every corner, every part of the coast, has been thoroughly searched, with the exception of the depths of Harrison's Bay, and there I should not think it likely they would go. The natives at Point Berens would have known it, had any one been there. The northern shores of Herschel Island I did not visit. At the time we were there it was blowing hard from NW, W, SW, and our time was getting very short. All marks on the coast and many poles have I seen and examined, taking us often very much out of our course, and giving us a wet walk. In fact, I fear to say there is but little hope of any news of our gallant countrymen, at least the way we have come, and none unless Sir James Ross gets any, or they return to England.

I have seen no difficulty in a proper ship getting on by the same route as we have come, and can hardly think there is not one deep channel into the Mackenzie, where such a rapid current is met with. Our boats I found very small for the voyage. If we could have kept the sea at times, we should have performed it in half the time. In the river work the men have been greatly at fault, particularly when we came to the tracking over large stones, our only way of getting on. We arrived here very weary, the gentlemen and parties at the different posts wondering how we got on, and expressing astonishment at our small and deeply laden craft. Nevertheless they did their work well, and I should have much liked to have got them home.

I have been obliged to draw largely on the Company's stores for clothes for my men; for such a ragged set as we were on arriving I have not for a long time seen. We all started with but little hope of getting thus far, and it was out of the question our taking much, with so much of other stores. I know there was not a blanket among the fourteen. But thank God, He has indeed been with us, and it is only by His help and assistance we are here. We are now waiting for the boats from the Great Slave Lake, where the men winter, and in June next all start for York Factory in the Company's boats.

On my arrival in England I hope to lay before their Lordships a track chart, my journal in full, with all notes and observations I may have obtained on this most interesting expedition. I cannot help recommending Mr. Hooper, acting mate and my second, to their Lordships most favourable consideration. He has been active and zealous in the performance of his duty; and all the dip observations along the coast up to the Peel were obtained by him.

I hope their Lordships will not think me presuming in taking the liberty of enclosing with this a letter to my wife, which I beg you will be good enough to have posted.

I have, &c.,
W.J.S. Pullen,
Lieutenant of Her Majesty's brig *Plover*,
Commanding the Boat Expedition.

To the Secretary of the Admiralty, London.[20]

Chapter Two

The Franklin Searches
of 1848 and 1849

Despite a great deal of effort and incredible hardship on the part of many brave men, very little had been accomplished by the three Franklin searches carried out in 1848 and 1849.

The expedition led by Captain Sir James Clark Ross, R.N., with H.M. Ships *Enterprise* and *Investigator*, was greatly hampered by ice in Baffin Bay in 1848, and eventually spent the winter at Port Leopold, which is on the north east point of North Somerset Island. In the spring of 1849, five search parties were sent off. Between them they searched the north and a part of the west coast of North Somerset Island, visited Fury Beach and Baffin Land, while one party crossed Barrow Strait and put up notices about food dumps. No trace was found of the Franklin expedition by any of these searching parties. In August 1849, Ross left Port Leopold, to try to reach Melville Island, on the north side of Melville Sound. The two ships became trapped in the ice in Barrow Strait, and were eventually carried out into Baffin Bay. By the time they were clear of the ice the season was far spent, and both ships returned to England, Ross reporting himself to the Admiralty on 5 November 1849.[1]

Sir John Richardson's overland expedition reached the Beaufort Sea on 3 August 1848, and turned to the eastward to search the coast as far as the Coppermine River. Stores of pemmican had been left at Fort Good Hope and Point Separation for the boat searching parties from *Enterprise* and *Plover*, together with instructions telling them where they should spend the winter.

71

Caches of pemmican were also left at Cape Bathurst, Cape Parry and near Cape Krusenstern. By 22 August, Richardson had reached Cockburn Point where he found the Dolphin and Union Strait full of ice. Conditions were so bad that further progress was impossible. The three boats had suffered severely from the ice and were now barely seaworthy. One was left with a cache of pemmican near Cape Krusenstern, while the other two found a resting place in a bay near Cape Kendall. As it was not possible to cross to Wollaston Land, Richardson and his party set off on foot, up the Coppermine River and across country to Fort Confidence. This outpost was situated at the north east corner of Great Bear Lake, and was reached on 15 September. No trace had been found of Sir John Franklin and his expedition.[2]

Sir John Richardson, Dr. Rae and a few of the men spent the winter at Fort Confidence, the remainder being sent off to the fish station at Big Island on Great Slave Lake. In the spring of 1849 both Richardson and Rae received letters from England, so it is probable that they both knew of the plans and sailing of Captain Sir James Clark Ross and his two ships.

In the Admiralty orders issued to Richardson, he was directed to search the coast from the Mackenzie to the Coppermine River, and then the western and southern shores of Wollaston Land.[3] If it seemed necessary to continue the search for another year, the passages between Wollaston, Banks and Victoria Lands were to be examined. There was now only one boat available at Fort Confidence to carry out the 1849 search. Rae, who was a much younger man than Richardson, volunteered to carry it out with a crew of six men.[4] This was agreed to by Richardson, who left the fort with the remainder of the party on 7 May 1849. He returned to England in November.

Rae's orders from Richardson required him to go down the Coppermine River and cross the Dolphin and Union Strait to Wollaston Land, and try to carry out the original orders from the Admiralty.[5] Rae knew that Ross intended to send a party to the Coppermine River if he succeeded in getting to Winter Harbour on Melville Island in 1848, and that he was to give them every assistance. On 9 June, Rae and his small party left Fort Confidence, and by 21 June had reached a cache on the Kendall River.[6] He encountered great difficulties with the ice, due to the lateness of the season, and found it impossible to cross the Dolphin and Union Strait to Wollaston Land. By 23 August it was time to go, so Rae and his party returned to the fort, arriving on 1 September.[7] Here he gathered together all the stores and instruments, abandoned the fort and set off for Fort Simpson, where he arrived on 26 September, just seven days ahead of Lieutenant Pullen who was on his way up the Mackenzie River from the Beaufort Sea.[8]

By the end of 1849 the Admiralty knew of the results of Ross's expedition into Barrow Strait. They also had Richardson's account of his search along the coast from the Mackenzie to the Coppermine Rivers. Nothing had been heard from either Captain Kellett or Commander Moore, who were believed to be somewhere in the vicinity of the Bering Strait. Their reports were received by the Admiralty on 22 January 1850, and from them they knew that Pullen was east of Point Barrow on 4 August 1849, on his way to the Mackenzie River. After consulting with Sir John Richardson, the Admiralty came to the conclusion that he had reached the Mackenzie and had joined Dr. Rae. This was confirmed when Pullen's report, written from Fort Simpson on 4 October 1849, reached the Admiralty on 30 April 1850.[9]

Soon after Ross returned to England, the Admiralty decided to send out another expedition to continue the search for Franklin. This one was to go by way of Cape Horn to the Bering Strait, and search eastward from Point Barrow. It was commanded by Captain Richard Collinson, R.N., in H.M.S. *Enterprise*, with H.M.S. *Investigator*, Captain Robert John Le Mesurier M'Clure, R.N., in company. The two ships sailed on 20 January 1850, and it was during this expedition that M'Clure discovered a Northwest Passage.[10]

On the very reasonable assumption that Lieutenant Pullen was with Dr. Rae at one of the Hudson's Bay Company's posts on the Mackenzie, the Admiralty was anxious that he should carry out a further search in 1850. They asked the Hudson's Bay Company to give advice, assistance and provide any stores or provisions that Pullen might need. The Admiralty's instructions to Pullen, together with copies of the reports from Kellett and Moore, and a copy of the orders to Collinson, were forwarded by the Hudson's Bay Company to Sir George Simpson, the Governor of the Hudson's Bay Company in Canada. They left England on board the British and North American Royal Mail Steam Packet Company's ship *Europa*, Captain E.G. Lott, which sailed from Liverpool on Saturday, 26 January 1850. She arrived at New York on 11 February, and the mail was delivered to Sir George Simpson at his headquarters at Lachine on the 13th.[11] He sent the orders off at once by "express", and they were delivered to Dr. Rae and Lieutenant Pullen near Great Slave Lake on 25 June 1850.[12]

Chapter Three

Winter on
the Mackenzie River,
1849-50

Lieutenant Pullen and the two Royal Marines, John Herd and Robert Tullock, spent the winter of 1849-50 at Fort Simpson. The rest of his party, five in number, were sent on to the Hudson's Bay Company's fish station at Big Island. This is at the western end of Great Slave Lake, where the Mackenzie River starts its course towards the Beaufort Sea.

Mr. Hooper with five men had been left at Fort McPherson when Lieutenant Pullen departed for Fort Simpson on 6 September. It was understood that they would spend the winter there, and rejoin the main body at Fort Simpson early in the summer of 1850. Several of the men were suffering from exhaustion, and Mr. Abernethy had frostbitten feet.[1]

Mr. A.R. Peers, who was in charge at Fort McPherson, returned to his post on 18 September to find his population for the winter had been increased by six persons. Supplies for this number were not available, so Mr. Hooper and his men left the following day, bound towards Fort Norman. They arrived at Fort Good Hope, where Mr. Adam McBeath was in charge, on 26 September. Here they rested for two days, and then set off for Fort Norman, accompanied by two Indian guides. They reached their destination on 6 November, being welcomed by Mr. H.E. Mackenzie,[2] who was in charge. Here Mr. Hooper met the two Indian guides who had gone up to Fort Simpson with Lieutenant Pullen. From them he learnt that most of this party were to spend the winter at Big Island. As a result, Mr. Hooper decided that his group should winter at Fort Franklin on Great Bear Lake.[3]

By 14 November the ice on the Mackenzie was strong enough to allow Hooper and his men to cross and set off for their winter quarters. Three of the Company's men and two Indian guides went with them. Mr. Abernethy was left behind at Fort Norman, where he spent the winter with Mr. Mackenzie. Mr. Hooper and his party reached Fort Franklin on 19 November.

By 8 May 1850, they were back at Fort Norman, getting ready to set off for Fort Simpson. Dr. Rae arrived from that post on 22 May, on his way to Fort Good Hope. Two days later Mr. Hooper and his men set off for Fort Simpson, where they arrived on 1 June.

Dr. Rae was back at Fort Simpson by 10 June, bringing with him the furs from the Company's posts on the lower river. Some days later the first half of the Mackenzie River Brigade left for Portage la Loche (Methy Portage). The second half, which included Lieutenant Pullen, Mr. Hooper and seven men, left on 20 June, with Dr. Rae in charge.

On 25 June, within one days' travel of Big Island, the brigade met two Indians in a canoe, with the "express" which Sir George Simpson had forwarded on 13 February 1850. Here were the orders for Lieutenant Pullen and his party to turn about and face another year in the Arctic, searching for traces of the Franklin expedition.[4] It must have been a bitter moment when he read the Admiralty letter, when all his thoughts and those of his party were "homeward bound". The letter stated that a further search should only be carried out if Pullen thought it practicable and his party was not too far south on its way to York Factory. There could be no doubt as to the proper course of action. They must turn and try again. The very natural disappointment, at least for Lieutenant Pullen, was tempered by his promotion to the rank of Commander.[5] Mr. Hooper was made an Acting Lieutenant, to be confirmed on arriving in England.

The brigade went on to Big Island, where the remaining five men were collected, and Commander Pullen broke the news of a further search to his men. They all volunteered without hesitation. Dr. Rae and Commander Pullen discussed the situation concerning boats, stores, equipment and provisions, and the employment of some of the Company's men as hunters and guides. An attempt was made to reach Fort Resolution at the mouth of the Slave River to collect a boat, but this was defeated by the ice. The brigade then halted at or near Hay River to reorganize itself. Dr. Rae cleared one of his boats and turned it over to Commander Pullen, so that he and his party could return to Fort Simpson. During this stay Pullen wrote an official letter to Dr. Rae, requesting passage for Mr. Abernethy and John Senior, Able Seaman, to York Factory and to England in one of the Company's ships.[6] These two men were now medically unfit for further service in the Arctic. Pullen also wrote two letters to the Admiralty, which Dr. Rae arranged to be forwarded to York Factory with the brigade. These letters were received in Whitehall on 17 October 1850.

> Great Slave Lake, Hay River.
> June 28th, 1850.

Sir,

I beg to acquaint you for their Lordships information that on the 25th. inst, while ascending the Mackenzie and within one days journey of Big Island on the Great Slave Lake, I received their Lordships despatch of the 25th of January last, and humbly beg to express my gratitude for their expression and token of approbation of my conduct.

With respect to the further search on the Arctic Coast, after mature consideration and consultation with Dr. Rae, I have determined on proceeding immediately to the coast in accordance with their Lordships' wishes.

I beg to lay before them a summary of my resources and arrangements for the expedition.

(1st, Boats.) The boats in which we accomplished our

first expedition are in a very shattered condition, as well from the severity of the past winter as from the injuries received during the trip. In fact one is utterly unseaworthy, and with her I propose patching up the other. With a large new boat of the Company's now at Fort Simpson, fitted and adapted for the work, to which end I despatched a messenger on the 26th inst, I entertain sanguine expectations of satisfactorily performing the required duty.

On my arrival at Big Island I assembled my party and acquainted them with the intended voyage, when they unanimously volunteered for the service. It was with great regret that I found myself obliged to exclude two of the party from accompanying me; Mr. John Abernethy, (Acting Second Ice-Master), who suffers from frequent illness, and is, I consider, unfit for so arduous an undertaking; and John Senior, Captain of the Fore Top, who has been suffering with a bad leg, supposed to be a chronic disease. Poor fellow, he was most anxious and willing to go, and would run every risk. I have therefore determined on sending them to England.

To render efficient my arrangements, I have thought it necessary to engage three of the Company's servants, viz, Neil McLeod[7] as steersman and fisherman at the rate of £4-10-0 per month; William Hepburne[8] and Jerome St George (dit LaPorte)[9], rated AB; their services commencing on the 1st July 1850, and ceasing, the two former, on the embarkation at York Factory, the latter on my arrival with party at Norway House. As regards provisions, stores, etc, Mr. Rae and myself considered it necessary to provide 30 pieces of pemmican and 15 pieces of dried meat, to obtain the former of which it would be requisite to proceed to Fort Resolution, as the lower posts could only supply two-thirds of that quantity. We accordingly proceeded for that post; but being today stopped by the ice for an uncertain period, I have thought it better, after again consulting with Mr.

Rae, to make up the deficit with dry meat, in preference to losing time; only preferring the pemmican from its better stowage and less liability to wet. I accordingly return tomorrow towards Fort Simpson.

At Fort Good Hope I shall endeavour to engage two Hare Indians as hunters and guides; one, who is there, having accompanied "Dease" and "Simpson" on their trips of discovery. These will augment our party to 17 persons in all, which will not be more than sufficient crews for the boats. I have made a demand upon the Company's stores for such articles of clothing and equipment as I deemed absolutely necessary, including a few presents for the Esquimaux, and possibly, for the natives of Wollaston, or Banks Land.

My present intentions are to proceed down the Mackenzie along the coast to Cape Bathurst, and thence strike across for Banks Land; my operations must then of course be guided by circumstances; but I shall strenuously endeavour to search along all coasts in that direction as far and as late as I can with safety venture; returning, if possible, by the Mackenzie or by the Beghoola, which the Indians speak of as being navigable, as its head waters are (by Sir John Richardson) only a nine days' portage from Fort Good Hope, to meet which, or a similar contingency, I take snowshoes and sledges, etc.

During the past winter I observed constantly with those instruments left at Fort Simpson by Sir John Richardson, and shall now retain them for a second series, trusting to their Lordships' approval of that measure.[10] I have made known to Mr. Hooper their Lordships' approbation of his conduct, for which he is deeply grateful, and I beg to again recommend him to their favourable consideration as a zealous and active young officer.

In conclusion, I beg to assure their Lordships of my earnest determination to carry out their views to the utmost of my ability, being confident, from the eagerness of the party that no pains will be spared, no necessary labour avoided, and by God's blessing we hope to be successful in discovering some tidings of our gallant countrymen, or even restoring them to their native land and anxious relatives.

I retain the report of my observations, Mr. Hooper's journal, and other matters, until I can present them in person to their Lordships, forwarding only with this my journal [Has not been received at the Admiralty] up to this period, and the lists of articles supplied by the Hudson's Bay Company to the two of the party who now proceed to England.

The mosquitoes were so thick when writing these letters, that I was obliged to keep my head in a gauze bag, and hands in strong leather gloves. I was occupied no less than six hours in what, at other times would only have taken one, so dreadful was the torment, not withstanding the gauze.

I have the honour to be,

Sir,

Your obedient servant,

W.J.S.Pullen,

Commander, R.N.

The Secretary of the
Admiralty,
London.[11]

Great Slave Lake,
June 28th 1850.

Sir,

I beg to acquaint you for their Lordships information that the bearer, Mr. John Abernethy, Acting Second Master, Ice, of H.M. Brig *Plover*, is the person I have sent home as sick, and unfit to accompany me on this trip to the coast;

accompanying is John Senior, Captain of the Fore Top, of the same ship, also sent home for the same reason. They await their Lordships orders.

I have the honour to be,
Sir,
Your obedient servant,
W.J.S. Pullen,
Commander, R.N.

To:
The Secretary
of the Admiralty,
London.[12]

Chapter Four

Fort Simpson to Cape Bathurst
and Return, 3 July to 5 October
1850

On 29 June 1850, at Hay River, Commander Pullen and his small party said good-bye to Dr. Rae and set off across Great Slave Lake for the Mackenzie River and Fort Simpson. This was reached on 3 July. Here a busy week was spent getting ready for the voyage down the river to the Beaufort Sea and eastward to Cape Bathurst and Wollaston or Banks Land.

The expedition consisted of Commander Pullen, acting Lieutenant Hooper, eight seamen, two Royal Marines, three Company's men and two Indians as hunters. Pullen obtained a large, new Company's boat, which from its dimensions was almost certainly a York Boat.[1] He named her the *Try Again*. The only other boat was the *Logan*, the one remaining gig whale boat, which was repaired as much as possible. Apart from the stores and provisions that were loaded, Pullen took with him the sextant, artificial horizon and chronometer which had been left at Fort Simpson by Sir John Richardson in the spring of 1849, and which Pullen had used during the following winter. He also took a Halkett boat.[2] This was an inflatable india rubber boat which had been used during the Richardson expedition of 1848, and by Dr. Rae in his journey down the Coppermine River in the summer of 1849. In a letter to Sir George Simpson from Dr. Rae, written on 29 July 1850, from Portage La Loche, he asked that "the Halkett air boat" be forwarded from Churchill.[3] This means that the Halkett boat brought back by Dr. Rae from Fort

Confidence in September 1849 was the one taken by Commander Pullen.

On 11 July 1850, Pullen and his party left Fort Simpson. They reached Fort Norman two days later and arrived at Fort Good Hope on the 16th. The next day Pullen wrote the following letter to the Admiralty, which they received on 24 March 1851. From this they knew that Pullen had their letter of 25 January 1850, that he had set off for Fort Simpson and the Beaufort Sea, and also that it was his intention to proceed along the coast to Cape Bathurst and then try to cross to Banks Land. Nothing more was heard from him until his report of this expedition reached the Admiralty on 22 April 1851.

Fort Good Hope, Mackenzie River,
July 17th., 1850.

Sir,

I have the honour to report for the information of their Lordships, a summary of my proceedings since the 28th. ultimo, at which date I had the honour of despatching my last letter by the H.B. ship from York.

I returned to Fort Simpson on the 3rd., inst., from which date until the 11th., my own party, as also the people of the Fort, were busily engaged in preparing the boats for the voyage, some of the blue jackets volunteering to act as carpenters, and handling saws and planes with nearly equal facility as the marlinspike. I have had the new boat (of which the dimensions are in the margin) fitted with two masts, fore and aft sails, and an iron keel-band.

Try Again, length 40 ft., keel 30 ft., beam 9 ft. 4 in., depth 3 ft. 2 in., masts 22 ft. She is certainly very large, but the only smaller boat there (built for Sir J. Richardson) is not of sufficient capacity to contain all our provisions and stores; and should we have the good fortune to discover the missing party, we shall be enabled to afford them more efficient assistance, although her size will entail on the party a little extra work as regards ice, portages, etc. The "Logan" was as thoroughly repaired and fitted as possible, and having received provisions, stores, etc, from Fort Simpson, we started from that post on the 11th instant, reached Fort Norman on the 13th, stopped there one night to receive the contingent of provisions and stores from that station, and arrived here yesterday morning, having pulled day and night (the wind being almost constantly fresh against us) with the exception of one or two trials of sailing, in which the "Try Again" (which name I have given to the large boat) answered as well as could be expected. We have here completed our supplies, amounting to 45 pieces, sufficient for 120 days for our party of 17. I intend also to take up the pemican buried at Point Separation, leaving a notice there, should any parties arrive and need provision, of the nearest post where they may be obtained, which I consider to be that on Peel's river, to reach which cannot occupy them more than three days at the farthest, although I do not consider it probable that any party can arrive, or at any rate before our return, when I shall if possible replace it. I have engaged here two Indians to accompany us as hunters, and made arrangements for others to look out for us on the banks of the "Beghoola" or "Inconnu," [Anderson River] should we ascend that river, which they say is seven nights from this, and well stocked with deer; but we should probably take a rather longer time to accomplish the journey across, as our men cannot be such expert walkers as those trained from their infancy to the exercise.

Should we fortunately attain Banks Land and find the sea clear to the eastward and a favourable breeze, I am led to suspect that we may possibly proceed to Port Leopold; but I only name this as a possible chance, should their Lordships not hear from me of our return this season. Again, could we only reach Cape Bunny with our boats, whence Sir James Ross turned to the south, we shall certainly not return, but proceed on foot, for which I think we cannot be better provided, all hands being equipped with dresses and mocassins of moose leather, than which nothing is better adapted to resist the icy blasts of the frigid north, requiring less under clothing, which should always be of flannel or woollens, except for the feet, duffle or blanket wrappers being far preferable to any kind of sock or stocking, and thus the men are less tightly and cumbersomely clad than with the usual provision of cloth garments, English Leather shoes, etc.

I have written to Mr Rae, requesting a supply of provisions, clothing, etc, the former to meet our wants in case of return by the Beghoola, and to carry us on to the wintering station, which the period of our arrival can only determine; the latter to repay our Indian hunters, who will not go further south, and such others as may assist us, for their services.

We are just on the point of starting, and I hope to reach the sea about the 23rd instant. Wherever I meet with remarkable headlands or points either on this coast or otherwise, I shall take care to have conspicuous notices of our visit, and perhaps a deposit of provisions. Our stock on leaving Point Separation will consist of 2,300 pounds of dry meat, and 1,700 pounds of pemmican; also half-a-dozen cases of preserved meat, which will remain so to the last.

Agreeably with the opinion expressed in the latter part of my journal, I do not think that Captain Collinson's ships will be able to get along the coast from Point Barrow, if they reach so far, unless the ice be further removed from the shore than at the time of our last voyage. The steam launch will have a good chance, as drift wood is plentiful along the coast east of Cape Halkett, and of course boats may again do what boats have done before.

The season has been extraordinarily fine, and our steersman (an intelligent man),[4] who was on the coast in both expeditions of Sir John Richardson and Mr Rae, is confident of an open sea. Others also, natives of the country, are of the same opinion.

Should I find provision and fuel plentiful on Banks Land, it is possible that I may winter there, for the further prosecution of our search next season.

In conclusion, I beg to assure their Lordships, that no efforts (as I before said) will be spared to endeavour to carry out their wishes to the utmost, and hope that the termination of this season may, by God's blessing, throw some light upon the whereabouts of the missing ships.

I have the honour to be,
Sir,
Your obedient servant,
W.J.S. Pullen,
Commander, R.N.
Commanding Boat Expedition in the Arctic Seas.

To:
The Secretary
of the Admiralty.[5]

Commander Pullen and his expedition left Fort Good Hope on the afternoon of 17 July 1850, and that night crossed the Arctic Circle once more. Point Separation was reached on 20 July, where pemmican left there by Richardson and Pullen was dug up, and on the morning of the 22nd the Beaufort Sea was in sight. It was entered by one of the western channels and after landing on Garry Island, they pushed on to spend the night on Pelly Island. The following day, after trouble with shoal water and a rising wind and sea, the party reached Kendall Island. On 24 July they landed on Richards Island, and by the following evening had got as far as Toker Point. Here they found Eskimo winter dwellings and caches of blubber and sea oil. Throughout their passage they were much hampered by shoal water, ice and foul weather. By the night of 29 July, Pullen and his little party had reached the western point of McKinley Bay, and here they were held fast by heavily packed ice, strong northerly winds, fog, and then heavy snow. The air temperature was down to 25° F, and conditions were thoroughly unpleasant. They were able to get away early on 1 August, but had to use axes, ice chisels and setting poles to make any progress. Throughout this trying and very difficult voyage, the Halkett boat was of great help in landing through the shoal water. Pullen mentions that on occasion as much as nine pieces (810 pounds) was carried in one load. By the evening of 3 August, after a great deal of difficulty with the ice, the party landed near Cape Dalhousie. The men were worn out and the two boats were in a shaky condition from their encounters with the ice. They were under way once more on the morning of 5 August, and that evening landed on Nicholson Island. The next day they reached Point Maitland where they met some of the Eskimo. Here they were held up by bad weather, and did not move on until the morning of 8 August. There were a lot of Eskimo about, who were very friendly, interested in the "Kabloonan", and prone to steal anything they could lay their hands on.

By the afternoon of 9 August the party had reached the Baillie Islands, and here they were brought to a complete halt by heavily packed ice which was visible from NW round through North to East. On 13 August, Pullen tried to reach Cape Bathurst on foot, but was prevented by a deep channel within four hundred yards of his objective. He waited until 15 August, hoping for a break in the ice, which did not take place. Had this occurred, it is probable that he and his men would have vanished into the Arctic, to be seen no more.[6] It must have been a most discouraging sight, having come so far under such difficult conditions. There was no sign of open water anywhere, and the ice which contained a number of bergs, was heavy field ice which had not been off the coast that season.

Pullen and his party set off on their return voyage, during the morning of 15 August, sailed across Liverpool Bay and spent an uncomfortable night in the boats, at anchor near Cape Brown. They were under way again the following morning, but had to land later on as the boats were making a lot of water. Here they were storm-bound until the 21st, when they were able to move on, reaching the western point of McKinley Bay that evening. The following day they reached Refuge Cove. On the morning of 23 August, they were under way again, making sail to the westward towards Richards Island, intending to pass to the northward of it, and west of Pelly and Garry Islands on their way to the Mackenzie River. Two islands were discovered north and west of Richards Island which were named Pullen and Hooper respectively.[7] Garry Island was reached on the night of 26 August, and the following day Pullen and his weary men entered the Mackenzie River. On 31 August, after much difficulty in finding their way through the confusing channels, Pullen recognized his old camp site of 27 August 1849, which established his position. Here the *Logan* was hauled up onto the bank and left to rest in peace. She was worn out and no longer seaworthy, having travelled many miles since leaving *Plover* off Wainwright Inlet on 25 July 1849.

Once again Commander Pullen found difficulty in getting into the proper channel of the Mackenzie. Eventually he found himself in the Peel River, so went on to Fort McPherson where he arrived with his party on 7 September. He was met by Mr. McKenzie, and, after getting mocassins for his men and some stores, set off once more on the 9th, spending the night at Point Separation. The expedition reached Fort Good Hope on 17 September, and Fort Norman on the 25th. in a heavy snow storm. Fort Simpson was reached on 5 October, and no doubt was a most welcome sight.

Pullen, Hooper and the two marines Herd and Tullock spent the winter at Fort Simpson, the eight seamen being sent to Big Island. The report of this abortive expedition was written by Pullen at the fort and dated 29 October 1850.[8] It was received by the Admiralty on 22 April 1851. During the winter Pullen rewrote this report in greater detail, and added to it in due course his account of the final journey from Fort Simpson to York Factory in the summer of 1851. That part of this second account, up to the end of 1850, follows.

Journal of the Proceedings of the party from the River Mackenzie towards Cape Bathurst in search of Sir John Franklin's Expedition, thence back again, and on to Fort Simpson and England, between July 1850 and October 1851. By W. J. S. Pullen, Commander R. N., commanding the Expedition.

On Wednesday the afternoon of the 17th of July 1850 we left Fort Good Hope, with still the same fine weather which had attended us, and anticipations (from such an early season) of success in our undertaking. About midnight we crossed the Arctic Circle, the boats driving with the current, with the watch only pulling to keep in mid-stream, while the remainder were endeavouring to snatch a little repose. In truth it was hard work, for with myriads of mosquitoes it was almost a matter of impossibility, then only in short and feverish dozes with heads wrapped in a blanket. Day or night made no difference to them, they were our eternal tormentors; and in no hot country that I have ever been have I found them so troublesome. In the daytime they were not our only pests, for the bulldogs (immense large flies) were almost as thick and troublesome with their sharp and poignant bite; so between them both we got but little rest. On the afternoon of the 19th several of the Louchoux tribe of Indians visited us as we entered their territory, and informed us of their having had a fight with the Esquimaux, wherein they had come off victorious. It took place in the vicinity of Point Separation, but understanding it to have been a mere Indian affair did not give it much attention, or land, as they were anxious for us to do, but proceeded on our way; and the next morning, the 20th, landed at the Point. Here we stopped just long enough to make final arrangements in the boats stowage, and take up the pemmican deposited by Sir J. Richardson and myself the two preceding years, which increased our stock of provisions sufficiently for every purpose; and on the morning of the 22d, at 8 o'clock, once more got sight of the Arctic Ocean. On leaving Point Separation I intended keeping the eastern channel of the Delta, but the steersman informing me that it was shoal I kept more westerly in a wider and deeper channel, which took us out much further to the westward than I had calculated on, and through new channels; however, as we were in good time, and the additional distance no detriment, I determined on passing outside all the islands. Garry Island was now in sight, we made for it, and with the assistance of a light westerly breeze landed thereon at 1 o'clock. While dinner was preparing I walked to the highest point of the island (the soil of which was pretty profusely strewed with flowers), and got a good view round. To seaward an unbroken line of ice (or from N. 78° W. to N. 30° E.) was visible, with a strong blink to the S.W. To the N.E. was clear open water, and towards the Pelly Isle, which after our meal we made for, under oars (the wind having failed), and at half-past eight we landed on its northern shore and pitched the camp.

Our sea voyage was now fairly commenced, and all felt a most sensible difference in the temperature since the morning; then almost a tropical heat; now the chilling cold of the Arctic Sea, with thick and wetting fog closing fast around us, so that we were again putting on the warm clothing so lately thrown off. At 11:30 p.m. the fog cleared off, and showed us the ice driving in fast for the shore with a moderate breeze from the north.

Tuesday, July 23d, 1850. — The morning was fine with the wind still northerly, and the ice making rapid approaches towards the shore; but as it was early I waited for a noon observation, which places the island further north than the chart. I make it 69° 35' 55" 4 N., and longitude 135° 26' 39" 6 W., the latter of which is pretty nearly the same as the chart. Our hunters had been very successful here, having killed no less than forty geese, beside numerous young ones, and thin as they were they made an acceptable addition to our stock of provision. But with our fishing we were not equally fortunate, not even a single one.

The wind was now rather fresh against us, making our progress under oars very slow, so that it was two o'clock before we reached the eastern extreme of the island, certainly not more than three miles from where we had encamped. Here, landing for dinner, I walked to the highest part, and saw the ice to the eastward still heavily packed, and entirely surrounding an island, for which I looked in vain in the chart; and as I had other business in hand than fixing positions, I contented myself with a bearing of its northern part (N. 24° E.) then returned to the boat and proceeded. Pulling close along the ice to the eastward we found it heavily packed, and trending to the S.E. enabled us to make sail, which brought us to a low, narrow sandy spit or island, extending about E.N.E. and W.S.W. The shoal water and ice obliged us to pass to the westward of this patch, its extreme point being about four miles distant from the eastern shores of Pelly Island. We then steered for Kendall Island, and after passing a small high island on our starboard hand, we landed at 8.30 p.m. on the N.E. point of the former; both wind and sea having increased so much that we were glad to get shelter, therefore encamped for the night. From the N.E. point of the island, which was high, I again saw the island observed from Pelly Isle, with no less than three in addition, almost in a line with it, and that on which we now are; the ice so completely surrounding all but one (the nearest) that to approach them was impossible, if I had even been so inclined. The extremes of the nearest island bore N. 37° E. and N. 42° E., from three to four miles distant. From south round to N. 62° E. was also land, which

I take to be the western shores of Richardson's Island. Midnight the wind freshened drawing more to N.E.

Wednesday, July 24th. — Weather fine this morning, but wind still fresh from N.E. with very little ice in sight, but a strong blink to north and N.W. As we could not make much progress under oars against such a breeze, after pulling out a little to windward we made sail, and until a quarter to six were beating against the wind which would occasionally lull, giving us a good opportunity of judging of the boat's capabilities under canvass, not of the first order certainly, but considering she had the "Logan" in tow I feel satisfied that she will perform every service required. About this time the wind was falling when we pulled up for the western shores of Richardson's Isle, and at nine landed, but not until after much difficulty, by reason of the shoal water.

Working across from Kendall Island, on standing to the southward we found the water very shoal, and when we saw the land in the same direction it appeared low, sweeping round in a deep bight, and connecting with Kendall Island. From Kendall Island there appeared to me a connexion, or at all events only a separation of low swampy land by narrow channels; and as we saw deer on the latter, one of which our hunters shot, (the remainder of the herd wading off to a low patch,) I think is enough for saying that they are connected; for a swim from Kendall Island to the main without some resting place would be a long one.

This landing place was the northern extreme of Richards Island, from which the N.E. extreme of Kendall Island bore s. 80° w., and there was a channel of about one mile wide, bearing s.E., apparently leading to open water, and formed by another large island to the north whose extreme point bore from us N. 17° E.

Here we were also successful in procuring a supply of fresh meat, for directly on landing the Indians were off, one soon returning announcing the joyful intelligence of a deer killed. Carriers were never wanted to bring in the spoil, who were soon returning with the denizen of the wilds, skinned and cut up in true butchers fashion, and ready for the cook's selection of the choice morsels. These were pleasing and most acceptable times to the men, for after such a long spell of fish diet, fresh meat was a treat to them, in fact to all of us. Queer beings they looked in their various costumes, crowned with the red cap, more like wild men of the woods than the natty man-of-war's man, but there was no help for it, all have now been so long from the ship, with but few clothes at starting, that they are glad to put up with what little they can get from the company's stores. Mr. Hooper and myself have nothing to boast of either, for between us and the men there is little difference in costume or fare.

At Kendall Island last night we found the rise and fall about a foot, here it appears less, not more than four inches, the wind influences it greatly. The water too is getting more the colour of the sea, for until this time it has been muddy looking, and quite fresh, now a little brackish.

Thursday, July 25th. — The wind this morning was from the S.W. a moderate breeze, and notwithstanding the chilly weather we were pestered with mosquitoes. At 7.30 we shoved off, and as I was not certain about where the channel (showing between the two islands) led, we ran along the western shores of the northern island, and at 9.30 rounded its N.W. point, which I called Kellett's Bluff, in remembrance of a kind friend, when a strong breeze from W.S.W. brought up with it a thick fog, holding up occasionally as if to give us a glimpse of our whereabouts, and showing that the northern face of the island was a range of high and steep cliffs, which there was no approaching for the breakers, extending some distance off the shore, and which appears to be a characteristic feature in all these islands whether the shores are high or low. Outside of us the ice was driving along in large and heavy masses, and what with it and the shoal water our eyesight was on a constant strain

to avoid either collision or getting on shore. Once, notwithstanding our sharpness, before we could avoid it we were in
the breakers and bumping on a sandy spit, but, thank God,
we were soon off again, and making rapid progress to the
eastward with the increasing and favourable breeze. At
10.40 the fog cleared a little, we could see no land, but were
running along a heavy pack of field ice, which at 11 bore
more to the S.E. At 12.30 it was so far clear that we got a
glimpse of the land, distant on our starboard beam, which
from its appearance I take to be the two islands east of
Richards Isle, and at 9 p.m. landed close to Toker Point.
Here were a number of winter dwellings, large cachés of
blubber and seal oil, with many articles of Esquimaux manufacture, of which the men would fain have taken possession had I not stopped them, and on leaving placed among
the things several small articles, as beads, knives, scissors,
etc., with a board of hieroglyphics intimating who we were
and whither bound. We had up to this time made a very
good run, and as the wind was still favourable, although
light, I determined on going on. The ice was plentiful
about, but not sufficiently packed to retard our progress;
the usual watch was set, although we had not much of
night, for the sun at midnight withdrew but half his diame-
ter below the western horizon, yet it was cold and chilly,
with a wetting dampness in the atmosphere, which made a
coil in the blankets not at all unpleasant, a stretch was out
of the question as room was not so plentiful. On looking at
the chart, and taking into consideration the short distance
to Cape Bathurst, I confidently expected that the 1st of
August would see us there; I little thought then such
difficulties would be met with, or that they were so near at
hand; but this is anticipating, I will therefore resume my
narrative. It was 10 p.m. when we shoved off with a current
evidently in our favour, and the weather beautifully clear.
Passing the bay east of Toker Point we grounded but were
soon off again, and saw that the bay was full of ice. At mid-

night the wind was light from N.W., and on the morning of the 26th we saw a heavy fog, banks rising up from the same quarter. At 2 a.m. we were obliged to bear away to the S.E. to clear the ice, and get into what appeared deep water near the land, then from three to four miles off. After steering this course for a short time we found we were hampered by a succession of shoal flats and loose ice, and were obliged to try back for a long way, when about 5 we got to the edge of the pack, and also stuck there. Meanwhile the ice (with the easterly current) having so closed in on the land, and still approaching it with no open water visible, that we had once more to break through towards the land to avoid being crushed, and succeeded in reaching the inner edge, now aground in one fathom a long half mile off shore. Here we held on for some time in hopes of a change; got breakfast, accompanied by a heavy down pour of rain, when seeing no difference, but indications rather of something worse, I reluctantly made for the shore, which after much difficulty, lightening our small boat and the aid of the India rubber canoe,[9] we succeeded in reaching, and set up the camp.

From the highest peak on shore there was no open water visible to allow of our proceeding; whichever way we turned, to seaward, presented an unbroken field of ice, excepting the narrow belt of shoal water between it and the shore, where before we had so much difficulty, and where in the gale which followed quantities were driven, and pieces so close to our large boat (at anchor) sufficiently large as to excite fears for her safety. As it was early in the day (only 9 a.m.) when we landed, with no hopes of getting on, the nets were laid out, and hunters sent off, who returned in the evening unsuccessful, but reporting the land we were on to be an island, with a wide channel between it and the main, and where we had already found was at the N.E. point of the island, deep enough close up to the beach for the boats, but shoal between it and where they were now lying. At 5.30

p.m. the wind came from east, and the tide was rapidly falling, so that at 9.30 p.m. our boats were very nearly dry. At 10 it came on to rain, and continued very heavy all night.

At 2 on the morning of the 27th our large boat was afloat, when she was hauled out into deep water, and at 4 we began getting our camp gear off, hoping for a good day (as the ice had driven somewhat off shore), and make up for our lost time of yesterday. The wind was light from east, with a dark gloomy sky and occasional drizzling rain, when at 6 in a heavy squall it shifted to north and put an end to our moving, for the ice was again driving in faster than ever, and the sea in a short time presented the appearance of one white mass tossing about in wild confusion with the gale, a thick fog coming in at the same time.

Fortunately for our boats a very narrow strip of sand (dry only at low water) outside them, preventing some of the larger masses driving in, and by the middle of the day the tide had risen so considerably from the effect of the wind that we were enabled to shift them to the north-east end of the island, where they lay in perfect safety. Our nets we were obliged to take up, finding in them four white fish and three flounders. We tried them at another place, but got nothing.

At this place we saw traces of Esquimaux, a deer pound of sods so placed as to appear like men, in a long line. All water we found was in pools, and very brackish, so we got our supply by melting the ice which was driven in on the beach. A few tufts of grass, plenty of moss, and patches of the small leaf swamp tea (in bloom), of most delicate flavour, but not a tree or a bush to afford us the least shelter from the piercing wind; and as neither of our tents (so completely worn) were proof against the heavy rain, hail, and snow which followed in quick succession, our position was by no means an enviable one. A quarter mile to the eastward of us were a few sand hills, so about noon of the 28th, finding it no longer bearable, each shouldered his share, and in spite of the heavy gale, and snow fast falling, we took up a berth under the lee of them, where our situation was in a short time certainly much improved, and we could stand to the fires and somewhat dry our wet garments; completely to do it was impossible, for the atmosphere was so loaded with moisture that anything exposed to it soon felt its influence. Towards midnight of the 28th the weather began to moderate, the wind now from W.N.W., but it was very foggy, with occasional showers of heavy rain. The thermometer throughout has been ranging from 32° to 31°.

On the 27th in a break of the clouds I managed to get the latitude 69° 44' 15" and a very imperfect sight for time, which places us in Hutchinson's Bay.

Monday, 29th July. — This morning the weather was rather improved, with the wind light from N.W.; the ice still heavy, but showing a few openings, so after breakfast, and embarking our camp gear, at 8.30 shoved off. As the tide had not receded much, we got over the shoal water in shore, and out to the edge of the pack, along which we pulled, having in many cases to lighten our heavy boat by means of the India rubber.[10] Our progress was by no means quick, for frequently we were obliged to push into the pack, and break a passage with ice chisels and axes before we could get along. This ice was heavier than that of the 26th, with much of its upper surface worn away, leaving long under tongues, which the weight of the boat alone frequently broke away; at last we got clear, this is into a wider channel, and with sails and oars made pretty fair progress until 1.30 p.m., when we took the ground. We were now about three miles from the land, and after in vain trying for deep water, I saw no other resource but to break through the outer pack, which was very heavy, field and hummocky ice, with open water outside, to all appearance deep and clear of shoals. The India rubber boat[11] was once more inflated and loaded; so after selecting the narrowest, and what I considered the most practicable part, at 1.50 we commenced, and not until 3, after receiving many hard rubs, did we get into the deep water, with no pack visible to seaward, but several bergs and large floe pieces driving down to the pack with the moderate N.N.W. wind. This pack followed pretty nearly the trending of the coast, and making sail we turned along its outer edge which we found getting much heavier as we advanced to the N.E.; fog occasionally obscured all objects, but as it cleared got glimpses of the low land and isolated peaks distributed along and seen from the coast, but a long way off. At 8.30 p.m. I saw heavy ice to seaward, which from its great height I considered to be the barrier, and not seeing a continuation of the open water concluded we had been running into a deep bight of the ice, which, if the wind came off shore, would place us in a very ticklish position, particularly as we had not seen any opening by which we might get into the land. On turning my attention to it I saw it looming through a light haze much closer to us than it had yet been since the morning, and on pushing into the pack found it to my great relief sufficiently loose to permit of our getting through by cutting and launching, accomplishing our deliverance by 11; and half an hour before midnight landed under the lee of a long spit of sand extending S.W. from the Bluff Point, forming the western horn of M'Kinley Bay. It was fortunate for us we got this shelter, for the ice on either side of the point was heavily packed, resting close in on the shoal water, with no prospect of a change unless the wind should shift either to S. or S.E.

The weather all day has been bitterly cold; our rigging on landing was encrusted with ice, and on visiting the many winter dwellings at this point, and which were apparently in ruins, we saw that all pools of water were frozen over, the thermometer standing 25° in the air, and 31° in the water clear of ice. In the afternoon we saw a fog bow, the clouds of fog retaining the form after the prismatic hues had disappeared.

Tuesday, 30th July. — The ice still heavily packed, and resting on the shoal water; outside was a few narrow lanes of open water; the wind from N.N.W. to north, with occasionally fog. At noon the fog cleared and the wind settled at north; the hunters were sent off and nets laid out, while Mr. Hooper and I employed ourselves in observing for latitude, dip, and variation; the men drying their clothes, provisions, stores, etc. In the afternoon the Indians returned with game (geese) enough for one meal, and three fish were taken by the nets. The ice unchanged, the wind moderate from north, the thermometer varying from 37° to 31°. At 11 p.m. it was low water.

Wednesday, 31st July. — This morning the wind was strong from N.E. by E., with much fog, and on reaching our observatory (the western horn of M'Kinley Bay, and the highest point) I saw no hopes of prosecuting our voyage, for although the ice to the westward had opened out into lanes, that directly in our track was still closely packed, resting on the shore, and stretching out to sea as far as was visible. This was indeed discouraging, for in the Mackenzie the spring had been so early and extraordinarily fine up to the very day we entered the Arctic Ocean that we all fully calculated on finding an open sea, and up to the first detention in Hutchinson's Bay made sure of being at Cape Bathurst by this time. We now see how little to be depended on are inferences drawn from such circumstances; already we have had much trouble and difficulty in getting thus far, and have fully experienced some of the severities of these regions. With the exception of yesterday, the weather has been bitterly cold, the ponds and sea close along shore showed this morning a coating of ice, and all the afternoon the snow fell heavily, now lying thick around us. This is now the sixth day of our detention, and as yet I see no possibility of our further advance. The thought is constantly presenting itself to me, that if we are thus enduring, what must be the sufferings of the gallant band we are endeavouring to find? May God in His great mercy direct us, and have us all in His safe keeping, for I feel fully that He only can help us.

It was high water this morning at 1.45, low at 11.30, showing a fall of sixteen inches, and at 5 p.m. it was high water again, the rise being only nine inches, the tide then standing an hour before falling. In the evening the wind fell, and if the many visits Mr. Hooper and I have paid to the look-out hill could have driven the ice off shore, we should have been far on the voyage ere this; but that barrier to our advance still stares us in the face, and appears that only a southerly wind will start. The thermometer this evening was 25°, young ice forming in all the pools sheltered from the wind (now from N.E. by N.), and number of snow birds about.

Out nets have been more productive than heretofore, yielding a dozen fish, chiefly "inconnu"; a young seal was also caught, but the man who visited them (the Canadian) got frightened (having never before seen one) and let it escape.

Thursday, 1st August. — This morning we found all pools hard frozen, much young ice close along shore, and the water left in our kettles last night was now solid ice; the thermometer at 8 o'clock stood at 29°. The ice was yet heavy, driving with the N.W. wind, but as there was open water showing in many places, I determined on trying to get on, and at 8.30 shoved off. After some difficulty in clearing the near ice lying aground on the shoal water off the front, we were enabled to make sail, and got a short and very circuitous run until 11 o'clock, when we were again having recourse to axes, ice chisels, and setting poles, to get along, in which arduous work we were engaged until the evening, when at 6.30 a heavy fog coming up, with many shoals as well as heavy ice in our track, I made for the shore, and after much difficulty succeeded in reaching it, landing on one of the islands S.W. of Cape Brown in latitude

70° 5' N. (about). Towards night the weather became dark and threatening, with thick wetting fog and occasional snow. The wind from north, thermometer 27°.

We have found the India rubber boat[12] of the greatest service, both in landing on these shoal shores and lightening our large boat to get over shoals; she has been laden with as much as nine pieces (equal to 810 lbs.) with which she swam very light. I have been paddling about in her, with two men and a boy in perfect safety, but I should say greater length would be an improvement.

Friday, 2d August. — This morning the weather was thick and foggy, with a light wind from N.W. At 8 the weather began to brighten up, and at 9.15 we moved on under oars. At 10 we made sail, the wind veering to the north, and were turning through a loose pack until 11, when we found it close in on us, and resting on such shoal water that inside it it was impossible for us to go; ice chisels, axes and setting poles were therefore in requisition again, and until 4 o'clock we were alternately pulling with that laborious work on a slow but onward progress. About this time we rounded the extreme of the shoal water off Cape Brown, and once more got into deep water. Our large boat as yet is quite tight, but they both have received so many hard rubs and severe squeezes that should we encounter much more of the same sort of work I fear they will soon be unserviceable altogether. From 11 until this time we had been out of sight of land; I now ran in for it, carrying deep water up to a loose pack stretching eastward, with its western extreme resting on the islands off Cape Brown, and as there appeared deep water inside this pack we forced through with but little difficulty, pulled between it and the land, occasionally grounding, when at 7 o'clock we landed on a small island on the western shores of the bay formed by Capes Brown and Dalhousie in latitude 70° 8' N., and encamped for the night. It was early certainly, but after such a hard day I found it necessary to stop to recruit my men. During the day the weather was gloomy and threatening with occasional drizzle and snow showers; the thermometer ranging between 28° and 25°.

Saturday, August 3d. — The weather this morning dark and cloudy, but every appearance of clearing. It was my intention to retrace my steps, and again get outside the pack we had passed through yesterday evening, thinking it might lead direct across this and into Liverpool Bay, as from our present position the ice appeared to lay thick in the bottom of this bay, rendering it very problematical whether we could get through it. It was noon before we started with a moderate breeze from N.W. (westerly), when after passing through a first pack on our backward route there opened out a wide channel leading east, to all appearances clear, and which I determined on following. We were soon under sail, with clear beautiful weather, and running with a fair wind on a course for Cape Dalhousie as near as was possible to keep it, considering the many loose pieces of ice in the way. At 2 we saw several large bergs lying on the edge of the outer pack forming the channel, the heaviest ice we have yet seen; and as from the boats I could not see any land or how the open water led, I landed and mounted to the summit of the highest, which was at least fifty feet above the sea. On such a slippery surface great ingenuity was requisite to keep one from quickly finding his way to the bottom, for, sailor-like, none of us had thought of bringing what was close at hand in the boats, and which would have aided us much, namely, the ice chisels; however we managed to get up, and were amply rewarded for our toil with a most extensive view. The deep channel we crossed yesterday led into that we were now in, which with many a tortuous course passed Cape Dalhousie, thence turned out to the northward and appeared to lose itself among heavy ice; between the channel and the shore was a dense pack of field and hummocky ice, with not a vestige of open water in it, and completely filling up the bay. Through this there was no hope of our being able to force a passage to get into Liverpool Bay, for to follow this channel with the certainty of its leading out to sea I did not think prudent, as we should stand a very poor chance of seeing the land again if a shift of wind to the southward should set the ice in motion, or even if it was to freshen up from its present quarter, and to turn back without another endeavour to get on I was very averse to; we therefore descended from our perch, and I determined to push on, at least as far as abreast of Cape Dalhousie, trusting that Providence who had brought us thus far in safety would not desert us in our hour of need. After filling up our kettles with water from holes in the ice we again made sail, moving among ice getting heavier as we advanced, and a little before 7 p.m. shortened sail abreast of the Cape, distant about a quarter of a mile, and from which we were separated by the pack, which at its narrowest and best part for forcing through that we could see from our mast-head was certainly not more than 800 feet. The wind was now quite light when at 7 we commenced operations, getting on famously for the first 50 yards among loose floe pieces, and which we managed to separate and break their edges with our setting poles, axes, chisels, etc., but after this it was a continued heavy labour, and only at 10 o'clock that we got to the inshore edge, with all hands so fagged and wet nearly to the middle that I made for the nearest land, where after our usual necessary practice of wading, making several trips with the India-rubber canoe,[13] etc., our camp was established by midnight, and all hands but one, the watch, were soon enjoying nature's best restorer. I have now seen more than 22 years of a sailor's life, and can safely say have never been engaged in such laborious and disheartening work as we have gone through this day and since the 27th. The thermometer this day ranging between 32° and 27°, and this evening as fast as we cut a channel the young ice would be making before we could fairly get through, and it was only by perseverance that we accomplished the job; we might perhaps have made it a portage, but from the nature of the ice our boats would have received more injury in launching, and we should have not got over in double the time.

My usual practice on landing was to take a view round from the highest point; on doing so here I saw that all outside of us, and stretching far into Liverpool Bay, was one vast field of solid ice, with a narrow channel of open shallow water between it and the land. Our encampment was on an island (Cape Dalhousie itself, in fact) inside of which was open water, but affording no passage for our boats. Resting completely on the cape (our boats lying just to the westward of it) was the ice, the large boat at anchor as close in as she could come; her bilge and sides, from her many encounters with the ice, as rough as a porcupine's back, and what was worse, much of her planking so separated from the timbers that one might easily pass the hand between some of them; in truth we now begin to find how weakly she is built, for on looking closely into her injuries we see how badly she is fastened, with nails not sufficiently long to clench or rivet, that I am astonished she has held on so well. Could I have imagined that boats for running rapids (often bumping over stones) were so weakly built, our carpenter (one of the marines) should certainly have put in and clenched a few additional nails before we started. Our own boat, the "Logan," is now in a most shaky condition, and so leaky that we can put nothing in her that will injure from wet, but she has had a long voyage before, so it is not surprising.

Young ice formed along shore of considerable thickness during the night.

Sunday, August 4th. — This morning the weather was quite calm, with a dark dull looking sky. There was no change in the ice, so I did not move on, particularly as I do not like doing more on the Sabbath than is actually necessary. At noon I read prayers to the party.

At 5.45 p.m. it was low water, and after rising 11½ inches

it stood at midnight; the ice at that time had driven more in, but the pack opening out and spreading.

Firewood we find here very scarce, in fact since leaving the Pelly Island it has been gradually on the decrease, and in several places we have had to take a wide range before obtaining sufficient for our wants. Since getting out of the influence of the Mackenzie this is the only place where we have found fresh water, getting our supply before from the ice.

This is now the 4th of August; from appearances there are yet more delays to be met with, and I begin to fear our expectations so frequently indulged in previous to entering the Arctic regions were too sanguine and doomed to be disappointed, and we may yet have to turn back without accomplishing even the small portion (to Cape Bathurst) of what we started for. After a long conversation with Mr. Hooper, and considering well our position, and the probable difficulty we may yet meet in our way, I have come to the determination that if we do not reach Cape Bathurst by the 10th instant to give up the idea of going to Banks Land direct so late in the season, unless from the state of the ice and fair winds I could make certain of meeting but few obstructions, and instead make the best of our way along the coast to the eastward, and push for Wollaston Land where first seen, thence on towards Banks Land as far as practicable, with the certainty of leaving our boats on the coast, if not before, and cross the ice to regain the continent. This, I think, we might easily accomplish by leaving the greatest part of our party on the main to await our return. Our course then to be for Fort Confidence on Bear Lake, where we should be almost certain to meet Mr. Rae, and equip ourselves with provision to take us to the nearest post on the Mackenzie. I consider this about the best plan to adopt in the event of the first failing, particularly as the steersman (M'Leod) knows the route; and provided as we are with sledges and snow shoes I cannot doubt of our being able to accomplish it; slow we may be, sailors are not generally good walkers, but as the journey has been done before I do not see why we cannot do it.

Monday, August 5th. — This morning was calm and cloudy; low water at a quarter after 6. After breakfast we embarked, and at 9.15 proceeded, threading our way through heavy ice and over shoal ground, on which it was resting, by means of oars and poles, into Liverpool Bay, when at 10.50 we got into deep water. Making sail to the light W. by S. breeze, we kept along the western shores of the bay from 1 to 2 miles off, just outside the shoal water; and, although the ice was still heavy, as we advanced south it opened out, and brighter prospects were dawning on us, when, having run a distance of from 9 to 10 miles from Cape Dalhousie, we landed on a low point to have a look round us. To the S.E. lay Nicholson's Island looming very high, with a comparatively open sea between us and it, which I purposed keeping; and after a slight dinner we proceeded, with a light N.W. breeze, which soon failed us; however, at 8.30 we reached the northern shores of the island, having passed much loose hummocky and floe ice driving into the bay; on the horizon it appeared thick and heavy. We passed a few grampus and small whales, also quantities of Esquimaux ducks. The water was deep; an occasional cast gave us mud, 4¾ fathoms, on the main shore, and 7½, mud, within a couple of miles of the island.

Here, as at almost every place where we have landed east of the Mackenzie, was shoal, so that it was some time before we got on shore, but as the temperature throughout the day has been warmer than usual, the thermometer in the air ranging from 37° to 29°, in the sea 36°, the wet walking was not so keenly felt. The camp was established on the beach, just at the point where the island begins to ascend, attaining to a moderate height, keeping nearly the same on the whole face of the eastern shore. The western shores are high and steep; and the whole island has the same general feature as all the lands of the Arctic sea, ice the substratum of a dark soil, thickly covered with a variety of mosses, and here and there short wiry grass. These cliffs plainly show their nature, for in many places the surface soil is washed off either by rain or thaw, like a land slip, when you see the main body to be nothing but ice. About our camp we soon found it out to our cost, and that frost was in the ground throughout, for the fires soon brought it out, making what we had thought perfectly dry as wet and mucky as if water had been just poured over it.

Among a few patches of grass on a light sandy soil we found plenty of mushrooms, which were a most welcome addition to our usual meal of the hard dried meat. Partridges were innumerable, but the hunters at first hardly thought them worth expending powder and shot on, so we only got a few.

During the night the thermometer in the air ranging between 33° and 41°, sea 34° and 38°.

Tuesday, August 6th. — The finest day we have had since leaving the river, and so warm that the mosquitoes paid us a visit. The thermometer at 6 o'clock in the sun 54°, at noon it was 78°. At 9 we embarked and pulled for Point Maitland, with a light air from E.S.E. We had now a very open sea, only occasionally passing a few pieces of floating ice; on the horizon, however, it was still very thick, with heavy fog banks accumulating and the mirage strong. At noon the wind drew to the N.E., breezed up, and made our progress very slow; and as we neared the land came off in such heavy gusts, that our large boat, from her light draft and extreme flatness, would do nothing under oars; we made sail, and only at 5 succeeded in gaining the beach. This was Maitland Island; the beach narrow, and of light shingle, backed up by high icy cliffs, with the usual coating of mud, making it appear at a short distance off as if it was really nothing but mud. As we carried deep water up to the beach we got the tracking line out, and at 8.30 rounded

Maitland Point; and for the first time this trip we saw Esquimaux; a single hut or lodge coming in view just as we were off the point. On landing we were received by two women (an old lady and her daughter), who seemed rather anxious for us to go away; but after getting a few presents, and finding us peaceable, were assured we should do them no harm; for as it appeared to be the most convenient place for firewood, now very scarce, I chose it for the camp. The old woman became very garrulous, examining everything, and as busy as possible, sitting down at the door of the men's tent, intently watching them arranging the interior. They told us the men of their family (eight in number) were away fishing, pointing to main land towards Cape Bathurst, and that there we should find many more "Inneet."

Our hunters were rather surprised at these women, never having seen any before; it could not have been their beauty, for neither of them had any to boast of; their dress was certainly different from their own women; but the low waddling square figure, long coarse grey hair, and bow legs of the elder dame was quite enough to attract the notice of any one, particularly with nothing in her countenance to indicate one of the softer sex; however, they were good friends in a short time, the gentlemen visiting them in their hut, and receiving presents of fish and other delicacies, etc. which they were as willing to bestow upon us all.

Wednesday, 7th August. — At 6 we were preparing to start with a fresh breeze from the westward, and had embarked the tents and other things, when a thick fog came on, which determined me to wait in hopes it would hold up. At 9 the weather was rather worse, with a heavy rolling surf on the beach, and much ice, so that I resolved on waiting for a more favourable time, rather than run for a dead ice shore; and as the boats were not in a very safe position they were hauled up, the tents again pitched, and the hunters sent off to try for deer, and being fearful of going by themselves, one of the men accompanied them.

113

The Esquimaux dwelling was on the beach just at the foot of the bank. I expect it was only a temporary affair, for fishing parties, as it was composed of nothing more than a few pieces of drift wood covered with sods and skins, with a scaffold close to, whereon fish (herring) were drying. In the course of the day we missed the women, and conjectured they had gone off to summon others who might be on the island; but they had left everything behind them, showing no fear of our attempting to appropriate any of their property.

On the hill just at the back of their hut were many upright posts, remains of old winter dwellings, and from which we got our chief supply of firewood. Whether these dwellings are inhabited every winter I cannot say, certainly not without much repair and preparation, for all that we have yet seen have been in a most dilapidated condition, with quite a ground floor of ice. In the evening the women returned again; and our hunters had been back some time without seeing any traces of game, but had shot a couple of partridges.

Thursday, 8th August. — The weather this morning was very much improved, but with a wet fog, a light wind from westward, and a dark dull looking sky. At 8.30 we embarked, and made sail to the northward. At 1.30 observed, on a low point of land for which we were steering, a large Esquimaux village, the people of which as we drew near came off to us, the men in their kyaks, the women and children in the omiaks, and we were soon surrounded by a very large concourse, all apparently friendly disposed and very glad to see the "Kabloonan" (white men). Among them we observed a great many beads and other articles obtained from Sir J. Richardson's party; and after a time M'Leod the steersman and one of the native men recognized each other, the Esquimaux looking thereat very much delighted. They accompanied us, very often getting in our way, pitching all things into the boats, deer meat, wild fish, furs, fish, etc., the kyacks hanging on by our gunwale, and making themselves troublesome with their kindness, but readily moving off when told, only for a time though, and in no instance showing hostile feeling; bartering bows and arrows, etc. for mere trifles; in fact, I think, they would have parted with every thing they possessed, and really seemed glad to see us. The ladies, in particular, were most uproarious in their welcome, and seemed half mad, and making signs which were not to be mistaken. One married dame was just on the point of sending her infant child, by her husband, for barter, quite in a state of nature, she was however stopped by our declining so burthensome an acquisition. All this time we were progressing (although but slow) under oars, and whatever feeling of distrust might have entered the breast of any of us at first, on being so sur-rounded, was soon entirely dispersed. I knew only at certain points they could approach us with our long sweeps out; and a sharp look out was all that I considered necessary for any emergency.

We were threading our way among heavy masses of ice, much of it close in on the shore; and the banks for a consid-erable way up faced with snow, which, together with the dark, gloomy, chilly weather, seemed to throw a damp over our prospects. The omiaks with the female part of our escort were now dropping off singly and returning to their village; when at 3.30 we landed in a small bay about 7 miles from Cape Bathurst, the Esquimaux men did the same, and while our dinner was cooking, an animated barter of fish, deer meat, bows and arrows was carried on until our meal was ready. After hastily despatching it, we shoved off again, and on drawing out of the bay, saw the omiaks coming after us again; we then learnt from the men, who knew how far we could go, that they all intended accompanying us, and those astern were their women, who they had sent back for the camp gear. This I did not exactly like, not being sure how long we should remain as friendly as now and they pointing inside the Baillie Islands as being the best course to pursue; I instead went outside, thinking by so doing we should get rid of them all, but we were mistaken, only a portion of them went with the women, leaving eight or ten men still with us, when at 8.30 p.m. we landed on the south-western shores of the western island, and camped for the night. Here the ice along shore was very heavy, lying close up to the beach, (which was steep too) and from our friends we learnt that to the eastward it was much thicker, and that we should soon be stopped. They remained with us all night, and were most friendly, but troublesome from their curiosity and obtrusive manner, and I fear, by the close proximity they appear so fond of, we shall have a share of those gentry they carry so plentifully about them; but that and much greater inconvenience would I endure, rather than give them the slightest cause of disagreement.

Friday, August 9th. — We took an early breakfast, and got everything into the boats, when so thick a fog came on, with the wind fresh from E.N.E., that I would not move on, particularly as there was so much heavy ice lying directly in our course. In the meantime the natives were walking about in friendly discourse, very much pleased with the trifling presents we had given them, and making themselves quite at home; one fast asleep in my tent, after asking and obtaining permission, while others were sitting round Mr. Hooper watching the pen as he wrote, and greatly surprised at the strange looking characters its movements made. At length, at 10 it partially cleared up, and we embarked, with the wind about N.E. by E., the Esquimaux trying all they could to persuade us from going on; I paid, however, no attention to them, thinking we might not only effectually get rid of them, but proceed on our voyage with more success than as yet attended us. Making sail we worked along shore, passing between many large pieces, when at 1.30 we were completely stopped by heavy packed ice, through which I saw no opening in the direction we wished to go.

This was in about latitude 70° 34' N., on the western part of the larger Baillie Islands; and not liking to go back we ran into a small sandy bay, only open to the S.W., with a channel of about half a cable's length between the shore and a large berg 30 feet in height, which with another, both aground, stretched completely to the opposite shores of the bay, and formed a good and snug shelter. On landing I walked to the top of the bank at the western point of the island, at least 40 feet above the water mark, and soon saw that unless there was open water between the islands and Cape Bathurst, our advance in every direction was stopped. From N.W. round by north to east, as far as I could see, was a dense field of ice closely jammed into the shore; when after walking along the bank for a couple of miles in the direction of Cape Bathurst, I saw no alteration, and returned to the camp, turning over in my mind what was now best to be done. In our former trip from Point Barrow to the Mackenzie I do not recollect ever seeing such large ice, excepting for a short distance in Camden Bay. This before us now was certainly not formed in one season on the coast, for it is in large, clear, clean, and glassy masses; I can only conclude that it has been driven from the northward last fall, and never since off the coast. I can now fully appreciate the information given by the Esquimaux, for they knew full well we should be stopped here; a number of both sexes joining us in the afternoon, having walked from their village, which they had established on the S.E. shores of the smaller island.

This was indeed a damper on our hopes of reaching Banks or Wollaston Land in this direction; for to be so effectually stopped from getting out to sea I never expected; but, from the many difficulties already encountered, only thought the barrier might check us, and then only well off the land, hardly thinking we should find the sea here less open than Sir J. Richardson did. I now resolved on retracing our steps in the only direction where open water was visible, pass inside the islands to Cape Bathurst, go along the coast, and endeavour to follow out the plan I had resolved on trying when at Cape Dalhousie, in the event of the first and main object failing. This latter course would be taking us to the southward again, and some success might yet attend us.

The thermometer during the day has been ranging between 35° and 34°.

As we were pulling in for the shore I saw a large bear trot off from the top of the bank; the hunters got out of the boat as soon as possible and gave chase, but as they were long in starting, and did not see him at first, lost the chance. Soon after the arrival of the first Esquimaux a woman came into the camp who had seen the animal on her way to us, and had to go down over the bank to avoid him, where she sunk nearly to her middle in the mud, and had a heavy and fatiguing walk; poor creature, she looked quite exhausted when she came in. Parties of both men and women were now flocking to us in numbers, but were quiet, and keeping a sharp look out for bruin. At last they discovered him, and with a shout pointed out his whereabouts, in the act of swimming in for the shore, at the opposite point of the bay to where we were encamped. All hands were now on the move, Esquimaux and white men starting off together, each with their own weapon of destruction, and a most animated chase took place. On reaching the spot he was making for, seeing so many foes, he turned about, and swam for a more distant landing, and directly on getting out of the water received a ball in his foot, which staggered him for a moment; recovering he again took to the water, making for one of the large bergs, and on his passage received a ball in the back of the neck, causing him to turn and grin on his enemies; at last he gained the berg. The Logan meanwhile had been launched, and was close at his heels as he got out of the water, but did not succeed in bringing him down, only worrying him until he took the water again, when another actor appeared on the arena, an Esquimaux in his kyak, who drove him fairly out to sea, inflicting many severe arrow wounds and otherwise annoying him, until the brute received the death wound from a musket ball lodged in his brain by one of the Logan's crew. He was towed to the beach, and really a big fellow he was. The Esquimaux who followed him so perseveringly (it had lasted about four hours) was rewarded with a broad dagger and several beads, greatly to his delight. It certainly was a most exciting scene, to see this man playing about the animal in his light and tiny craft, driving his arrows into him, throwing water into his face with the paddle as he turned on the canoe, and keeping just out of his way as if it was a matter of every-day occurrence, showing ready tact and great coolness, for the least blow of the brute's paw (whose endurance was truly astonishing) on the kyak would have upset her, and nothing could have saved the man from the infuriated animal.

All this we could see from the bank, and he certainly would have escaped if it had not been for the Esquimaux. As soon as the animal received his death wound, a chief who was present exclaimed that it belonged to the "Kabloonan"; but not wishing to keep the whole, I had it cut up, and retained the skin, with the smallest half.

Here we discovered how frightened our Indians were of the Esquimaux. One of them really could not sleep all night, and was constantly asking the men on watch why they did not awake me up, and get ready for the attack he was sure was meditated. Their reason for so thinking I could not find out, for our visitors were as quiet as possible, and I am sure had not the least idea of anything of the sort.

Saturday, August 10th. — The wind still the same as yesterday, and as I saw no change in the ice, embarked at 9 and ran along the land to round the south-western point of the island, when the wind was unfavourable for Cape Bathurst, and as it was blowing fresh we landed at 2.30 on the main, in the same bay we had been once before. We were now joined by a small family we had not seen before, a man and three women; we made them a few presents of beads, and essayed to improve their beauty with vermilion, they offering no objection, on the contrary desiring it. The youngest of the women (apparently unmarried) was certainly not a bad looking girl, who after receiving her quantum of decoration on her face, was dragged forward by her female friends, who turned up her frock, patted her belly, and requested a like operation might be effected there; they were gratified, Mr. Hooper daubing it to their hearts content. After dinner the wind still fresh against us, we shoved off again, and made sail to beat up for Cape Bathurst inside the Baillie Islands. As we drew toward the cape the wind fell, and we were again under oars, pulling about a midchannel, the shoals from the main extending nearly that distance to the Baillie Islands. At 8 p.m. we saw the village of our friends situate on the smaller island three or four miles from the cape; as we drew near we counted twenty-two lodges, which poured out their numerous inhabiters to look at the strangers. They were soon off to us, shouting and making noise enough to deafen one, but all in high glee. Some of the old men came alongside, and told us we could go no further, and from the look of the ice we were beginning to be of the same opinion; but as there was nothing like judging for oneself, we pushed on, they leading the way, sounding with their paddles, and took us round the spit stretching to the westward from the cape, through the nearest channels formed by the ice in the deepest water, and as far along its northern shore as we, or they could possibly go, which was not half way between the extreme point of the spit and Cape Bathurst, where a number of winter dwellings were situated. It was now evident that our advance in every way was stopped, and that no cutting or portages would avail us here, for the ice was close in on the shore stretching far into Franklin Bay, out to seaward as far we could possibly see, and in my firm opinion never off shore this year. This opinion was confirmed by the Esqui-maux, who, as far as we could understand, had not been beyond this with their canoes this season. Again, the strong westerly wind which blew all the 7th not appearing to have affected it, was more confirmation of my opinion, and that we could do nothing with it. Strong winds I have always found more destructive to ice than anything else, therefore more welcome to the voyager than calms; but here it appears to have worked no change; certainly it did not last long.

This complete check was a great disappointment, the more keenly felt, as never hoped for. I made certain we should pass the cape when we came in from the Baillie Islands, and get along the coast without difficulty, from the very circumstance of Sir J. Richardson having done so in 1848. M'Leod, the steersman, who was one of his crew then, was astonished, repeatedly saying they never met such ice in the whole course of their voyage. To go back again, directly, I did not like doing; to remain here was out of the question, for there was no firewood, and I was unwilling to encamp among so many natives, now about us, who, although apparently friendly, are most expert thieves, in which art they have been already exercising their ingenui-ty, one fellow slipping a silver spoon up his sleeve, another burying a frying-pan, and our pockets frequently tried, so that it was very necessary to be ever on the watch. In an attempt to reach the cape, on the southern side of the spit, and encamp there, we failed, from the shoal water extend-ing a considerable distance off. I therefore determined on returning to the bay where we had dined, being the only place where we could conveniently land, establish the camp, and wait until the 15th, and if no change took place in the ice by that time, return as fast as possible to the Mackenzie. Under existing circumstances, I consider this about the best thing to be done, for if we remained longer, and the ice should open out, it would be too late to go northward, or even to reach Wollaston Land by the coast, and a sacrifice of time, stores, and provisions, without any resulting benefit; the same also would be the case if we returned by the "Inconnu" river.

We did not get to the camping ground until midnight, our friends leaving us as we passed their village, thinking, I expect, we were taking our final departure, but on running down the coast, the family who had visited us at dinner time, and were encamped at a short distance from our resting place, observed, and let the others know of our whereabouts; however, we were free of them for some hours, and got a quiet night.

In the early part of the day the weather was dark and cloudy, but towards noon it cleared, and the sun shone brightly, with the wind, however, fresh from N.N.E. coming over the ice, and a low temperature; we felt the cold severely. All along the main shore, as well the sea-face of the islands, from as far west as Pelly Island, we have found abundance of snow lying, particularly on the high and steep banks.

Sunday, 11th August. — At midnight the thermometer stood at 28°, with a thick frost on the ground, and the wind moderate from E.N.E.; this morning it was from the same quarter, so I remained in the camp, and, as far as possible, kept the day in peace and quietness. At noon we offered up our prayers of thankfulness to our Heavenly Guide, for the protection He has given us in our perilous voyage. The weather warmed a little towards noon, the thermometer getting up to 43° in the sun, and 36° in the shade; at night it was down again to the freezing point. In the evening several natives came into the camp, among whom was a chief, with his three wives and family; they pitched their tent close to ours, and were quiet and orderly.

Monday, 12th August. — Blowing hard from E.N.E.; and as this was a wind not likely to move the ice I did not leave the camp. After breakfast the nets were set, and hunters went off to try for game. All day Esquimaux came flocking in, and by the evening we mustered a strong force of both sexes and all sizes, very friendly, but without exception the most persevering pests I ever met with, picking up everything they could clap their hands on, and shoving their noses everywhere, but displaying no hostility, on the contrary showing every inclination to assist, such as fetching wood and water, etc.; and indeed we cannot move a step without being followed by some of them. Our dresses are great curiosities, both men and women handling us most annoyingly. I have not been sparing of presents to either men, women, or children; and the poor creatures are highly delighted with the most trifling article; but to get a knife appears to be the height of their ambition. I think we have really gained their friendship; bows, arrows, dresses, in fact any and every thing, they are most willing to part with, and appear to have every confidence in our good faith towards them, the women and children coming to us alone without the slightest doubt or hesitation. Mr. Hooper has got from them a number of words, by which means I think we may form a pretty tolerable vocabulary; there appears to be little difference from the western tribes. About noon our hunters came back with only three partridges; they went off again in the evening, taking merely their guns and ammunition, and entirely of their own free will, notwithstanding their fear of the Esquimaux.

Tuesday, 13th August. — The wind this morning was from the north, with heavy fog banks on the horizon. Our hunters had not returned. At 9, they being still away, I determined to go on to Cape Bathurst again with only one boat, and leave Mr. Hooper with the other to await their arrival; desiring him to go some distance back from the coast and make musket signals occasionally, in case they might have missed the camp. When I shoved off the greatest number of the Esquimaux accompanied me, leaving as we passed their village on the island. At 1.30 I landed once more on the spit, just in the same place I did before, and found the ice quite unaltered from its state of Saturday night. Being anxious to get to the cape if possible, I walked towards it with two of the men, but when within a couple of cables length of it we were stopped by a channel of deep water which we could not pass, and the ice was not sufficiently near to walk on; thus were we cut off from the desired goal. The open water south of the spit, which we had tried on Saturday night, would not allow of the boat coming any nearer, so whichever way we turned obstacles not to be overcome met us, and return was all we could now do. We got back to the boat, and at 3 p.m. shoved off again, pulled to the N.E. point of the small isle, and from the high bank had a most extensive view of the ice. From N. 71° 30' E. to west, the sea was completely covered, with not a vestige of open water to be seen, excepting a few pools a short distance from us. There were many high bergs in the pack, which was chiefly composed of heavy field ice, and, as I have before remarked, has never been off the coast this season. With the wind from E.N.E. we now made the best of our way back to the camp, with sorrowful hearts at the disappointment of hopes from which we had expected such favourable results; and on reaching the camp at 5 p.m. found a further disappointment as well as painful anxiety about the Indians, for they had not returned; neither had Mr. Hooper, who had been some distance back from the coast, found any traces of them.

How to account for the absence of the Indians in any other way than that they had deserted us, (from their fear of the Esquimaux,) I could not. They of late had been making repeated inquiries as to the direction and probable distance of the "Inconnu," as well as the direction and distance of the Mackenzie from it. Turning over these circumstances, I concluded they had gone off for the former, and would easily find their way to the latter river, as one of them had hunted on the banks of the Inconnu before, but had never got so far north as to be clear of the wooded country. From his account deer were most plentiful in the neighbourhood; ammunition would therefore be all they wanted, of which their pouches were nearly full when they started. As for Indians losing themselves in a plain country like this, I hardly thought possible; but as they had gone off without any spare shoes or tobacco, the latter of which an Indian will never be without if he can possibly help it, was rather against their having deserted; at all events, I resolved on waiting until the evening of the 15th.

The account of the Inconnu from the Indian who had hunted there before was somewhat different from what we got at Fort Good Hope. His name is "Karias," and was one of the party from whom Mr. Hooper in 1849 had taken a guide when on his way after me to Fort Good Hope. They had just then (the Indians) arrived on the River Mackenzie from the Inconnu, having been eight days on the journey. It appears that the Indians call it "Soon illay thess," or Unknown River, as it is in the French. They laughed when we gave Sir John Richardson's word "Beghoola," which they said signifies "no meat." "Karias" drew a sketch like this:

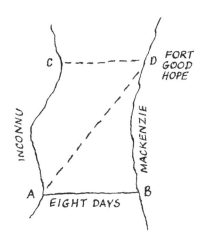

From A to B, C to D, is full of large lakes, so cannot well be travelled. From A to B is the road they took heavily laden, which occupied them only eight days. B to D is only a two days march along the banks of the Mackenzie to Fort Good Hope, or three at the least. He thinks our boats might go up to A; the current is sluggish, and the water may be deep enough, as higher up than where they cross it is up to a man's middle; good tracking ground, and deer as thick as mosquitoes.

Wednesday, 14th August. — This morning the weather was very fine, with the wind moderate from east, thermometer standing at 39° in the sun. No signs yet of our missing hunters. At 9 I sent Mr. Hooper with two men out once more to search for them, but he returned at 2.30 without finding any tracks. Many Esquimaux had arrived during the day, and now mustered stronger than they ever had before; they encamped near us, and were friendly as usual, but most confoundedly troublesome, craving after everything they saw, and using every artifice to possess themselves of it, requiring the eyes of an Argus to watch them. I was now getting seriously alarmed about our Indians, for even if they had made for the "Inconnu" it is hardly possible they would get to it without meeting strange Esquimaux, and there would be no knowing the consequence. My reflections were indeed painful, particularly as the time I had fixed on for our return was drawing near, and longer delays might be dangerous. With the wind as it was now, and no prospect of a change, the probability of getting round Cape Bathurst in any time to be of service in the main object of the expedition was very small. I was restless and uneasy, and could not remain still in one place for a minute, when I walked to the bank on the south side of the bay, and took a long and anxious look over the wild and dreary plain, when to the southward apparently close to the bank were two objects apparently sometimes advancing and then receding very slowly, and strangely distorted by

mirage. I could not make out what it was; at last concluding it some of the Esquimaux, never thinking the Indians
would come from that quarter. I once more returned to my
tent, when to my inexpressible relief, at 4 p.m. the two missing ones came in. Poor fellows, they made a sad appearance, weary and exhausted, with hardly a rag on their feet,
having been on the tramp ever since they left us, wandering
about in search of the camp.

The night they went off they wounded a deer, and in the
ardour of the chase had got so completely bewildered as to
their locale as to despair of ever finding us again. In the
course of their wanderings they came on the shores of
Franklin Bay, and found the ice there in the same state as
at Cape Bathurst. On asking them what they would have
done if on their return they had found us gone, they replied
that they should have dug a hole, laid down in it, and died.

After the Indians had recruited a little, I determined on
shifting the camp, and at 5 began to embark the gear, when
the Esquimaux, thinking perhaps it a fine opportunity, and
that from their strong muster they might appropriate things
with impunity, made several daring attempts at embezzle-
ment, one fellow cutting very expertly the knife lanyard
round one of the men's waists and walking away with the
knife with all imaginable coolness. However, by much for-
bearance and a sharp lookout we managed to get everything into the boat without loss, or giving any cause for
disturbance of the friendly feeling which had throughout
existed. As a farewell present I gave them a quantity of iron
hoop; and at 5.30 we made sail, ran along the coast to the
southward, and at 8 landed about five miles from the old
camp, at the place where we first saw these people, and for
the last time were joined about an hour after by two women
and seven men of the number we had been so long amongst,
who were apparently determined to see the last of us. One
of the Indians who had throughout been in such a constant
state of fear now made sure, although we were the stronger

party, that they were bent on mischief, and in spite of the fatigue he had undergone latterly could not sleep a wink all night.

Thursday, August 15th. — Wind moderate from eastward this morning; and as it was the day I had fixed on for our return, there being no visible signs of change of wind to affect the ice, we embarked at 8 a.m., previous to which I made presents to the natives who were with us. It is true they had before received some; but I wished these to be a mark (the most acceptable to them) of our sincere friendship, and gratification at the manner in which they had behaved while we were among them. They all appeared delighted; and the eldest woman made a long speech as we were shoving off, the purport of which, as far as we could understand, was, that they hoped the "Kabloonan" would come amongst them again. We made sail directly across Liverpool Bay, encountering rather a heavy sea particularly as we neared the western shore, and shipping much water, to the damaging of our provision. We made the land inside Cape Dalhousie, but could not get on shore, for there was too much surf beating on the outlying shoals. Hauled out, passing many pieces of drift ice, and at 3.20 rounded the Cape, and kept on a s. westerly course. When at midnight, after making several ineffectual attempts, by consequence of the shoal water, to get on shore to encamp, we gave it up, anchored inside the shoals off Cape Brown, and slept in the boats. During the day we observed much large hummock ice on the horizon, and in the afternoon passed quantities of loose ice, with a strong blink from w. by N. round by north to s.E. At 9 p.m. the thermometer stood at 36° with a light westerly air.

Friday, August 16th. — At 8 a.m. we made sail, after having pulled well to the N.E. to clear the shoals. The breeze was fresh from the eastward. When at 9 we found we were still inside the shoals, and were once more obliged to take to the oars. With the fresh breeze we made but very slow work

128

of it, and it was not until 1.30 p.m. that we succeeded in extricating ourselves; then only by hauling the boats over the narrowest part, with the water just about to the men's knees. These shoals were not all dry, as laid down in the chart, for it was only an occasional patch that we found above water, or we might have got clear sooner. Outside the shoals the ice was heavy, in floe pieces, following the line of shoal, and distant from one to two miles off. At 4 it was quite calm. When, on looking into the well, we found the water above the ceiling, and, as the boat had been pumped out dry in the morning, concluded she must have started something coming over the shoal, although there were other reasons sufficient for such an increase of water, the oakum having worked completely out of many of her upper seams, and the second plank from the gunwhale, nearly fore and aft, separated widely from the timbers. We could put nothing in the small boat, nor was she in any way repairable, and I fear we shall hardly get her to the river. Her sternpost is nearly out, the knees of sailing thwart gone, with several timbers sprung.

At 8 we landed in latitude 70° 4' (about), where we had once before stopped (on the 1st). Immediately cleared the boats, and found, as I feared, much of the provision wet; but as the spot was a good landing place, with a very long and wide dry beach, I determined on waiting to-morrow, and have a regular drying match. The hunters were sent off directly, and at 10 one returned for assistance to bring in the deer he had killed, which was most welcome news, for all hands were complaining, and I knew not what to attribute it to, otherwise than the provision, for it certainly is wretched stuff.

Saturday, August 17th. — Heavy rain all night, with wind from the westward. At 9 it held up, but a thick fog was banking up to the s.w. Our boats were lying close to the beach; the camp was on a high bank; between them the flat dry sandy beach, of about a quarter of a mile wide, whereon the provisions were spread, and as the fog, which at 1 p.m. closed completely around us, was not damp or wetting, we had partially succeeded in drying all. At 5 the wind settled at N.E. by N. moderate, with clear weather; and as to-morrow was Sunday, I determined not to move on, therefore had the provision gathered together under the oil-cloths for another drying previous to putting it into the boat. The hunters were again successful, having killed a doe and her fawn; but our nets yielded only four fish "inconnu"; certainly a poor return, but two of them were the largest I have ever seen. The rise and fall of the tide was 13½ inches.

In the afternoon I took a walk, and a wet one it was, towards one of the many hills which are interspersed here and there along the coast eastward of the Mackenzie. From the summit of this hill I had a most extensive view. Sweeping round with the glass, to seaward, and not very far off, was still heavy ice; on the landside, a dreary desolate plain, cut up with lagoons and swamps, apparently only frequented by deer in the summer season. I saw four grazing in undisturbed solitude. The only dry ground appeared to be in the vicinity of our camp, and that of no very great extent.

Sunday, August 18th. — This morning the sky was overcast, and raining hard, with a moderate wind from N.E., but hauling gradually round to south until 8 a.m., when it settled at S.W. by S., and blew a gale, bringing up a thick wetting fog. We were now obliged to anchor the large boat off clear of the surf, and at 4 take up the nets, for heavy ice was driving in from seaward. Prayers were read in the morning, and afterwards all were anxiously watching the progress of the gale and rising of the tide, which by 6 p.m. had increased so much that we were all obliged to sally down to the beach and bring our provisions up on the bank, and had only just completed the work when the spot was covered to the depth of two inches; the ice, too, coming in still faster, and gale increasing.

Monday, August 19th. — No hope of moving, for it is now blowing hard from s.w. by w., with cold, wet, miserable weather. At noon it came on to snow; the tide still rising; ice covering the whole view to seaward, and exciting great fears for our large boat. In the evening the gale was still on the increase, with heavy squalls and snow. On opening a bag of pemmican which was rather damp, found it quite mouldy and unfit for use. This is not the first time such has been the case.

Tuesday, August 20th. — This morning the "Logan" was driven close into the bank by the tide, which had risen so high that all the flat beach was completely covered. Still blowing, but not quite so strong, now from w. by N. About 9 a.m. the "Logan" was able to get off to the "Try again," and found her lying very snug, the heavy ice being aground outside, and forming quite a breakwater, very much to my satisfaction, as I had been momentarily expecting to see her driven in on the beach. Throughout the day we have had rain, snow, and sleet at intervals, with the thermometer standing at 28°. In the evening the wind moderated, and the tide fell off the beach so much that we were enabled to load the boats ready for a start in the morning. Hard frost all night.

Wednesday, August 21st. — This morning the wind was moderate from w. by N., with a dark cloudy sky and heavy fog bank to seaward, the ground white with frost, thermometer at 6 a.m. 28°. At 9.15 we shoved off under oars, occasionally sailing amongst a loose pack. At 2 p.m. we landed by Bromell's Cove for dinner, and were visited by an Esquimaux family, who were most importunate for knives, needles, etc., in which particular their desires were gratified. At 3.30 we shoved off again, but were obliged to retrace our steps for some distance, having got inside a long spit of sand in the fog. Outside this spit the ice was lying thick and

131

heavy, apparently in the same state as when we passed this way before; and the wind having now shifted, we ran among it under easy sail, as the fog was very thick around us. At 8 p.m. the fog cleared, and finding we were nearly abreast of a former encampment on the point of M'Kinley Bay, we ran for it, hauled inside the spit, and landed for the night. The fog did not keep off long; just time enough to show us the heavy ice, then closing in thick and wetting, very cold and miserable. Thermometer 26°.

Thursday, August 22d. — A very thick fog this morning, with a moderate breeze from the northward. Our friends of yesterday visited us again this morning, and as my servant was clearing up the tent ready for embarking, the Esquimaux, who was watching him, abstracted the knife from his belt. Fortunately Mr. Hooper saw the fellow do it, and made him return his booty, which he did with a laugh, but evident disappointment. At 9 we embarked, and proceeded under oars, for the fog was too thick to allow of making sail. When at 10 it cleared a little, and we got under canvass, steering about south, with a moderate easterly wind. At noon the fog began dispersing gradually; We got sight of land. In half an hour it was quite clear, and we found ourselves in an open sea, with only a few pieces of drift ice here and there. At 2 p.m. we passed the winter dwelling we had landed near on the night of the 25th of July. They were then uninhabited; now several natives were there, perhaps preparing them for the ensuing winter. Many of them shouted, and waved clothes to us from the roofs, as a signal to land, but we were too anxious to get on. One man endeavoured to come off, but was either frightened of us or the sea, which was rather rough for his tiny craft, and put back again. At 6 we landed close to some other winter dwellings (farther south), to look for water, but finding none proceeded until 7 p.m., when we put on shore for the night on the northern side of Refuge Cove, and encamped. At 9.30 two natives were seen approaching, but were evidently in a great state of alarm; for what reason I know not; and it was long ere we could induce them to come into the camp; then only by assuring them that in the morning they should each have a knife, which they appeared most anxious to get. Wind light during the night from E. by N. Thermometer standing at 37°.

Friday, August 23d. — Directly we began to move this morning, and get our things into the boats, the Esquimaux scampered off as fast as they could; and it was only as we were going to shove off that they again made their appearance; not, however, venturing near, nor being without their bows and arrows. As I wished to assure them we were friendly, I walked towards them alone, with two knives and other trifles as presents; but it was long before they would come near enough to take them, and then again running off as fast as their legs would carry them to a safe distance. It was 7.30 a.m. when we made sail, with an easterly wind, for the opposite shore (Richard's Island), which we could only see from the highest hill at the back of the camp. As we drew towards the land, saw that it extended to the northward. We hauled out for the extreme point, and coasting along passed a deep bight or opening, showing like a channel leading through to the westward, and which bight I take to be the eastern extreme of the channel I had before observed from our encampment on Richard's Island on the night of the 24th of July; making, therefore, this new land an island, and a big one too, and which I now named Beaufort Island, after the Hydrographer of the Admiralty. We ran along the eastern shores of the island (which was deeply bayed), and before reaching its northern extreme saw another island, still more northerly, not so large, but forming a channel of at least 3 miles wide leading to the westward. This channel we ran through, keeping close along the northern shores of the large island, which was also deeply indented, and high steep muddy banks. At 2.30 we attempted to land, to get a few bearings, to show the position of these new lands; but from the heavy surf on the shoals, which appear to girdle all these islands, we did not succeed; therefore, held on our course, keeping as close as the breakers would allow. When at 6 p.m. we managed to get on shore, and encamped for the night on the western shore of Beaufort Island. Towards night we had very heavy rain, and a strong breeze from E.N.E., which at midnight increased to a gale, and seemed very likely to cause us another detention.

Saturday, August 24th. — Blowing strong from N.E. by E. About noon it moderated. We embarked, and made sail to the westward. As we drew off the land, we felt the wind more forcibly, and found the sea very much heavier than I expected; but as one of the new islands we saw on the 23d of July was directly in our track to Pelly Island, I determined on landing on it. Our first effort, on a narrow beach, under a high bluff (S.E. point), was unsuccessful, from the shoal water. We then ran for the dry patch extending from the southern part of the island, where we managed to get on shore by wading through bitterly cold water for at least a cable's length of distance; but any port in a storm, for it was now blowing a complete gale, and this was the only shelter we could get. On the beach, under the lee of a very high grassy bank, we just got room enough to pitch out two tents, and were soon again a little comfortable, with all hands running about to get warm, and firewood, which was very scarce. My intention, before I got on shore, was to land the provision, as from the quantity of water we had shipped it was again very wet; but as it would have kept the men too long in the water, and such a scarcity of firewood, I abandoned it for a fitter opportunity. In the evening the wind was a little more moderate; the sky dark and cloudy, with thick misty weather. At the back of the camp the ground rose almost perpendicular to a height of at least sixty feet. From the summit, for a short distance, was quite a table land then dipping to the N.E. for half a mile, when it gradually rose until you attained, about the centre of the island, not more than 120 feet above the sea. From this point, eastward, the land was gently undulating, and terminating in the steep cliffs of the eastern shores of the island to the westward, sloping off gradually to the beach. The greatest length of the island was, from N.E. to S.W., from three to four miles. It has the same characteristic feature as all lands of the coast, — mossy and swampy, except the face of the steep bank at the back of our camp, which had a thick grassy sward; and where we found plenty of mushrooms. In fact, it appears to be the summer side of the island, for some of the flowers we have already found were growing in abundance. Fresh water was most plentiful; but we had to go some distance for it.

S.W. of our camp were two small islands, close together, and not more than a quarter of a mile off, but surrounded with shallow water.

Sunday, August 25th. — Wind from N.E. by E., blowing fresh, with an overcast and threatening sky. At 11 a.m. read prayers to the party. In the evening rain, snow, and sleet. Thermometer + 29°.

Monday, August 26th. — This morning, about 3 o'clock, it was high water, when I had the "Try again" (our large boat) taken off into deeper water, to ensure our getting off in time; notwithstanding which it was past noon before we could move, so much time being taken up in embarking the camp gear, by having to make so many trips over a long stretch of shoal water. Early in the morning it was snowing very heavily, completely covering the ground; but in the course of the forenoon it ceased, and in the break of the clouds I managed to get a glimpse of the sun. The noon observation was pretty good, but those for time so imperfect that they cannot be depended on; neither is the chronometer to be trusted; and as the longitude I give from observation was from the error taken from a single lunar observation at the entrance to the river seven days after, I am more inclined to trust to the bearings and distances run, supposing the positions of the Pelly and Kendall Islands to be correct.

Camp on S.W. point of Discovery 1, or Hooper's Island, latitude 69° 39′ 21″ N., longitude 135° 2′ 28″ W., deduced from lunar; 134° 55′ 0″ deduced from bearings from Pelly and Kendall Isles. From this, bearings and distances place the centre of Pullen's Island in latitude 69° 45′ N., longitude 134° 30′ W.; the most northern land we discovered.

It was at noon the last trip was made; and at 12.30 we made sail with a fresh breeze from N.E. by E. We ran rapidly to the westward, passing outside the narrow spit or low isle before observed, outside Pelly Island; rounded the N.W. point of Garry Island, and at 7 p.m. landed on its south-western shores for the night. During the night we had both rain and snow. Rise and fall of the tide about fourteen inches.

Tuesday, August 27th. — This morning all pools of water were quite frozen over. At 7.45 we embarked, having the satisfaction of again stepping from the beach into the boats, instead of wading through bitter cold water. Firewood, too, was also plentiful, of which we took every advantage, by keeping blazing fires all night.

We steered about south with a light N.W. wind, and at 9 a.m. we were once more in the muddy and fresh water of the Mackenzie. At 11 we got into shoal water, and although far distant from the shore we experienced a continued succession of grounding in nearing it. At length we got into a deeper channel, which I was in hopes led into the river; but from the slack current, and slow advance, from meeting so much shoal water, I resolved on landing as soon as possible, to examine whether it was only a deep bight into which we were pulling. This we accomplished at 5, on the northern shores of this indentation. Walked a little way along the bank, and plainly saw that it was only one of the numerous outlets for the spring flushes of the river, as there was but

Captain W.J.S. Pullen, Royal Navy.

H.M.S. HERALD AND PLOVER IN BEHRING'S STRAIT.

H.M. Ships *Herald* and *Plover* in Behring Strait.
(National Maritime Museum)

Mr. William Hardisty at Fort McPherson, 1849.
(Hudson's Bay Company)

Legend: "H.M. Ships *Herald* and *Plover* with the Yacht *Nancy Dawson* off Wainwright Inlet. The boats under the command of Lieut. Pullen leaving for the River Mackenzie, and in search of Sir John Franklin and party. At 11:45 on the night of the 25th of July 1849 *(Department of National Defence)*

Plawson" off Wainwright Inlet — The Boats under the Command

ie, and in search of Sir John Franklin and party

ight of the 25ᵗʰ of July 1849

A York Boat. When the wind was fair,
a square sail was hoisted, sweeps were shipped,
and the "captain" steered with the rudder instead of
with the long sweep protruding from the stern.
(Hudson's Bay Company)

Dr. Rae's Halkett Boat.
(Hudson's Bay Company)

Dr. John Rae, F.R.G.S.
(Hudson's Bay Company)

little wood on the shore, the country very flat, and bearing indications of recent inundation. Flocks of wild geese were numerous, but our hunters were not particularly successful in shooting many, from the difficulty of approaching them near enough.

Wednesday, August 28th. — A slight frost this morning, with beautifully clear weather. At 6.50 a.m. we embarked, and proceeded under sail with a light wind from the eastward, steering off the land to clear the shoal water, as I had determined on proceeding westward, and enter the river by the same channel I did last year, which I knew to be deep. About 8 we rounded what I considered to be the outer part of the shoals, and finding deeper water, with a current setting off-shore, hauled in once more for it. At 9 we entered a narrow deep channel, and there being a strong current against us, I supposed we were fairly in the river; and as our provision was still wet, not having had an opportunity of getting it on shore since the last drenching, I landed at 10, to take advantage of the fine weather for drying it, as we might not have such another opportunity. Some of it we found in a very bad state from the wet. Here I got observations, which place us to the westward of Ellice Island; but as no land appears there in the chart, I conclude this to be land not before seen, and mean to follow through the channel which is formed by another island to the westward, yet whereon our hunters are now in chase of wild geese and swans. In the evening they returned with a few game, but that they had seen the big water from its western shores. In the afternoon Mr. Hooper and myself walked to a hill about two miles S.E. of our position, and from its summit plainly saw the Richardson Mountains, and deep indentures to the eastward, which I conclude to be a passage between this and Ellice Island.

In the evening light passing showers of rain.

Thursday, August 29th. — At 8.25 we embarked, and with a moderate breeze from the eastward made sail, following the course of the channel (trending south), with a light current against us. About 10 a.m. the channel began to open out, and we soon got into an open sea, instead of being in one of the numerous passages which led directly into the river, as was my conjecture yesterday. I still held on the same course (south) as near as possible, when we soon sighted land, which could be no other than Pitt Island. We ran for it, with the intention of passing along its western shores, thence to Colville Island, and the Man-of-war Channel; but the water was so very shoal, that, after trying in vain all day to get to the southward, both near and far off the island, I was obliged to give it up, retrace our steps to round the western part of the island, before we could get south. We had got so confused among the complete labyrinth of shoals, that it was with the greatest difficulty we got clear again before dark, and then only after lightening our large boat by a sacrifice of about 320 lbs. of meat. However, it was a good riddance, for it had been so often wet, and latterly so long, that it was so bad as to be quite unfit for food. At 10 p.m. darkness was closing fast around us, and as the shore was too shoal to approach (the N.E. part of Pitt Island) we anchored the boats, and passed the night in them; obliged to go hungry to sleep, as unfortunately we had no wood to make a fire, and, with the heavy rain which had been pouring for the last six hours, we were not very comfortable.

Friday, August 30th. — Early this morning the wind was rather fresh from N.N.E.; the sky looking dark, and threatening with rain. At 4 we got under weigh, and pulled along the N.E. shores of Pitt Island. At 7.15 observed a narrow channel, with a strong current setting into it, which led me to suppose that it might be a passage through the island. We therefore followed it, and at 7.30 landed on its western shore, not only to get breakfast but a warming, after the chilly and unpleasant night we had passed. It was still raining hard. However, we managed to get a fire, and partially dry our clothes. When before we had finished our breakfast, the clouds began to break, the rain ceased, and weather bid fair to be fine again. At 9 we embarked, and still followed the narrow channel. When at 9.20 we got through, and once more into open water, with the Richardson Mountains very distinctly visible to the southward. Steering in their direction, for the water was still very shoal to the S.E., at 2.50 we saw Tent Island, and at 4.30 came close on it, about 5 miles S.E. of its N.W. point. We now hauled to the S.E., keeping close along shore, crossed the channel between Tent and Colville islands, and at 6 landed on the N.W. point of the latter, and encamped for the night. Since 5 o'clock the wind had been strong against us from the eastward, against which our large boat made but little way with oars.

For some time I was quite at a loss here, thinking we had hardly yet reached Tent Island, for the coast is so totally different from the chart that I get puzzled; for although we came along this shore last year, I either could not have observed it so closely, or my memory is very treacherous. At all events, many of the party recognise it, and I shall keep on as we are going, as tomorrow will decide it.

Saturday, August 31st. — At 7.30 we embarked, and with the wind from N.W. ran rapidly along the land, steering east and S.E. by E. When at 9.37 we passed our old camp of August 27th, 1849, in latitude 68° 49′ N. All doubt of our whereabouts was now fully dispersed by the recognition of this spot. The only difference, easily detected, was that the water was higher now than then. Steering confidently for the Man-of-War Channel, we soon entered it, passed quickly through into the western branch of the Mackenzie, and at 1.15 p.m. landed, and encamped on the left bank of the river, in latitude 68° 44′ 25″ N., longitude 135° 44′ 42″ W., by lunar observation.

Here our provision was once more landed to be dried, for such was the shattered and leaky state of our boats, together with the heavy rain of the 29th, (against which our oil-cloths were but little protection,) that everything was again wet. Our large boat, with only a slight ripple of the water, would make as much as 70 gallons in the 24 hours. The small one we could put nothing into, and as she was totally unfit for repair, I determined on leaving her here. By this means our progress up the river would be greatly accelerated; and as, from the severity of the weather of late, and generally throughout the voyage, there was every likelihood of an early closing-up of the river, the sooner, therefore, we reach our winter quarters, the better. The small boat was cleared of everything likely to be of use, hauled up on the bank to her last resting-place, after so ably performing her arduous work, and on Monday morning, the 2nd of September, we began the ascent of the river.

On the morning of the 4th of September, wishing to avoid, if possible, getting into the Peel, we took a narrow channel to the left, hoping thereby to get sooner into the main branch of the Mackenzie, but the next day we again got into the channel we had been trying to avoid. However, the hunters in this very channel shot a moose deer, which sufficiently compensated for all disappointment or any increased distance to our voyage. On the morning of the 7th we passed a narrow channel on the right bank which led into the Mackenzie, and which we ought to have followed; but from the circumstance of the current running contrary to what we expected, and none of the men recognising it for the usual route taken by the boats passing from the Peel into the Mackenzie, we kept on, and only discovered the mistake when we got into the long reach of the former river, at the head of which Fort M'Pherson is situated. This was annoying, as it took us out of our way, and lengthened the voyage very much, which in these regions is of great consideration, and more annoying as the two men of our crew, old servants of the company, and had frequently passed through this channel, did not recognise it, and were hardly to be convinced when we got into the long reach, where the rest of us immediately recognised trees we had marked in 1848. One thing, the features of the river were altered much, by its being higher and broader than last year, and shoals dry then were now completely covered. As we were so near the fork, and all hands in want of mocassins, I went on to it, and arrived at 9.30 p.m. where we were welcomed by a Mr. M'Kenzie, in charge of the establishment, in the absence of Mr. Peers. We remained here until Monday morning, the 9th of September, when, after getting the necessary supplies, again proceeded; passed into the Mackenzie, and at 8.50 p.m. stopped for the night at Point Separation. Just before reaching the point, we passed the spot where a most cowardly and cruel massacre was perpetrated by some of the Louchoux Indians on a small party of Esquimaux. There was now only remaining to tell of the fearful deed the skeletons of the four kyaks of the unfortunates, and numerous footprints.

This affair we first heard of on our way down the river in July from the Louchoux themselves, but thought it was a fair stand-up fight by their telling; but at the Peel station we got the particulars from one of the white men present, and which I have given here as taken from his lips.

This man, Neil M'Kay, was one of a party proceeding in a small boat from Fort Good Hope to Peel's River. His companions were Manuel Herbert (a Canadian, and steersman in charge), Sanderson, and Brown, with two Indians (of whom "Maccaconce," who was on the coast with Dease and Simpson, was one). He, M'Kay, said that they were going down to Peel's River in the boat early in June 1850, and having been stopped by the ice near the site of old Fort Good Hope for two days, were short of provisions, and had thoughts of opening the cache at Point Separation. Having found geese, however, they did not do so, but landed as near to it as they could for the ice which bound the shore, to have a look at the "lobstick" [a tree with nothing but a few of its upper branches left remaining, the lower ones having been all cut off, so as to render it a conspicuous object], at M'Kay's request, he having never seen it. They beached the boat about a gun-shot below the point, and just then espied an Esquimaux in his canoe coming in and along through the ice, then another, and so on, until ten were counted. Manuel was about to fire at them; but M'Kay twice or more times turned away his gun, and entreated him to withhold until they should prove hostile in intention. Manuel consented to reserve his fire until M'Kay should run back a little way to see if a band of Louchoux, whom they expected, were near; and at a little distance he found, and told them what was the state of the case, when, as he says, they could not go fast enough, but barely hauling their canoes on shore ran along to the spot. The Esquimaux chief, or eldest of the party, told them to put down their guns, which they did, and he fixed all his arrows on the shore within a small circle, after which he held up his bow and empty quiver, to show that he had nothing more. Each of his party followed his example, after which a trade was carried on between them, buttons, knives, etc. being bartered for bone and ivory trinkets, skins, etc. When the trade began to slacken, two of the Esquimaux went off, to bring up the larger boat, with the women, peltries, etc., and these not returning speedily, two more went off to hasten them. There were now only six Esquimaux remaining, and all unarmed, while the Louchoux were fourteen in number, and the company's party seven, having in all seventeen guns among them. The Louchoux, being apparently apprehensive of the others going off, invited them to come on shore while waiting for the boat, and have a dance, which they did, but on the opposite side of a small creek. The chief first landed, pulled off his frock, and appeared in nothing more than his breeches and moccasins; then held up his hands and slapped his body, to intimate that he had no concealed weapons. His companions did the same, in succession, and each party began to dance on either side of the creek. Presently M'Kay observed one of the Louchoux skulking round the ice, trailing his gun after him at full cock. He made him take it back, and gave him a good scolding, and going back to the bank saw all the other guns at full cock. He afterwards saw some of the Indians going round by the willows to get behind the Esquimaux. There he stopped; but observed again, that, while half were danc- ing, to occupy the attention of their victims, the other half were stealing round to get in ambush. He spoke to Manuel Herbert to help him in preventing this treachery; but he replied that if they wanted to kill the Esquimaux he should not stop them, but would rather push them on, and that it was no business of theirs, etc. M'Kay now went to one of the Louchoux chiefs, and told him that Mr. Peers (the compa- ny's officer in charge at Peel's River) would be very angry if they killed the others. He replied that they would not fire at them, and M'Kay thought that he had stopped all murder- ous intentions. The other men, Sanderson and Brown, had made a fire at a short distance off, and did not at all come near the scene. M'Kay had slipped into the water while bartering with the Esquimaux, and being very cold, and now satisfied that no evil was intended, ran off to the fire to dry himself. He had not reached it, however, before he heard a shot, then another; and before he got back again "the place was all smoke," and four of the poor deceived Esquimaux lay outstretched on the ground. The other two got off to their canoes before the second volley was fired, but were both wounded by it. They nevertheless got away. Manuel had also fired among them, but said that he killed none. The Louchoux now fired arrows into the four, and one, who had only been wounded, got to a piece of drift wood in the water, under which he dived as the arrows came at him. They at length finished him with their guns, and he sank. The other bodies they cut under the arms, and laid them over their heads; also otherwise gashing and mutilating them; then left them, and went on to Peel's River station with the whites. When they all arrived at the fort, and the Indians there (Louchoux) heard how the affair had occurred, sided with M'Kay in blaming the perpetrators, who now said that they were sorry they did not take his advice, and should have done so, but that they *were pushed on by "Manuel."*

Such is the account given by M'Kay, who appears to have done all he could to prevent the cold-blooded murder. This account was confirmed by Manuel himself, whom (by permission of Mr. Peers, in whose boat he was steersman,) I questioned, on meeting them shortly before we reached Fort Good Hope. He admitted having fired three times at the Esquimaux, and that he replied to M'Kay to let the Indians do as they pleased; also that M'Kay tried to stop them. When asked his reason for his conduct, he said that he feared an ambush.

I can now account for the fright of the two men we saw in the vicinity of Refuge Cove, and consider that we have been most fortunate in not meeting any at the mouth of the river, where they generally muster strong. Had we taken the eastern channel of the river, and met them in force, where, from the narrowness, they would have had every advantage, we might probably have had to fight a great part of the way, if not the whole, to Point Separation, and perhaps not without serious loss.

I do not doubt that they will find means of paying off the score, and make no distinction of whites or Indians, particularly as some of the former were amongst the party, and aiding in the act.

On meeting Mr. Peers and party on their way to the Peel, they did not appear to be in a very prepared condition for resisting any attack, near as they were to Point Separation. At Mr. Rae's request, communicated by Mr. Peers, I handed over to him all our muskets and ammunition, taking his receipts, instead of carrying them to Fort Simpson, where we should have eventually left them.

I consider that by this unfortunate affair a good opportunity has been lost of establishing a friendship with the Esquimaux, had they been taken on to the fort, instead of so cowardly butchered; for it is evident they came for peace and barter, from the circumstance of their having women with them. Now, as at any time, when we have parties in the vicinity of and even among these people, it is particularly unfortunate, for the affair will soon spread, and the western Esquimaux are a more determined set than any I have yet seen.

Tuesday, September 10th. — After making a deposit of pemmican of ninety pounds in the same place the former had been buried, we started with the tracking line, keeping the left bank of the river for a short distance, to make up for the downward set of the current in crossing to the opposite bank, and moved on, dividing the crew into parties of four, each taking hourly spells. As the wind was strong against us, we did not get on very fast; but, taking all things into consideration, twenty-five miles a day I consider a pretty fair average; and we reached Fort Good Hope on the morning of the 17th. Here I found a supply of pemmican and flour, together with a few suits of clothing, which were issued to the men as far as they would go. I discharged the Indians who had accompanied us, paying each 120 skins, at the rate of 2s. the skin, and returned a quantity of dried meat. Mocassins we were in want of, for a great part of the supply we had started with was of such inferior leather that a day's tracking would wear them out. Mr. M'Beath had nothing in store but deer-skin, and those very bad. However, we could not go without shoes, so we were obliged to take them; and there being only two Indian women at the place to make them up, it was the 19th before they could get a sufficiency ready for us to start with, so we moved on, and having a passenger, an Indian woman, employed her to keep up the supply.

On the morning of the 25th, in a heavy snow storm, we reached Fort Norman, and as the weather continued bad all day I did not go any farther; but the next day proceeded, and on the evening of the 5th of October arrived at Fort Simpson. Chief trader Bell was in charge, who gave us a hearty welcome, and handed to me their Lordships despatch of the 3rd of May 1850, acknowledging the receipt of my letter announcing my arrival at this place in October 1849.

Tokens of the approach of a speedy closing of all navigation are very rife. Nature had donned her winter garb, for snow is lying thick around us, and the air is getting cold and frosty.

Between the entrance of the river and Fort M'Pherson on the Peel we had a succession of heavy rains, thence on to this snow storms, with very little intermission of fine weather, and a very low temperature, the thermometer on two occasions as low $5° +$. All the small streams were hard frozen, with ice in many places driving along shore. In the Bear Lake River it was thick, quite sufficient to check the progress of any boats that might be going in that direction. Many wild fowl were so frozen that they could not take wing as we approached them.

I found stowed here (Fort Simpson) for our use sixteen bags of flour and fifteen of pemmican, which, together with what I got at Fort Good Hope, makes eighteen of the former and twenty of the latter. I also got at Fort Good Hope a few other articles, such as tea, sugar, and biscuit, with a small quantity of wine and brandy (two gallons of each), which Mr. Rae wrote for last year on my first arrival. These are what the company call luxuries; and in a supply of provisions are never considered or sent for men in their employ, and at one time (a short one too) but sparingly for the officers; however, now I believe they are getting a little more liberal with the tea and sugar. On the coast we had but a small supply of any, and that only through Mr. Rae's kindness, it being a portion of his supply remaining. To the want of it, (which to us are indeed necessaries,) together with the badness of much of the provision we had, I attribute all the sickness we were troubled with. For myself, nearly the whole time I was ailing I could hardly ever keep anything on my stomach, and frequently troubled with flux of the worst description; and it was only after reaching Fort Good Hope, where I got a change or rather an addition of diet, in the shape of biscuit, flour, tea, etc., that I began to amend.

On the 18th of October I sent the steersman with ten men off to the Company's station on the Slave Lake, to pass the winter. Mr. Hooper, the two marines, and myself remaining here. The party for the lake were supplied with pemmican and flour for use, until they could get nets made and in order for service; and as last year they had but little fresh meat, I arranged for their getting an Indian hunter, adding powder and shot to what we brought back in sufficient quantity for the season. At Fort Norman Mr. Rae had left three dogs for our use, which the men took on with them, with permission to get others if actually necessary.

The clothes I found here, together with those at Fort Good Hope, were very short of being sufficient; there was a coat, waistcoat, and trousers, shirt, and handkerchief for each man, but what all most needed was very short; in fact, drawers there were none, and only seven flannels; and as the Company's stores contained none of those necessary articles I was obliged to take white cloth as a substitute, and blanket for wrappers for the feet, in lieu of the socks certainly not adapted to resist the cold of these regions.

I think this is likely to be a severe winter on the coast, from the early setting in of the cold weather, and consider that we were fortunate in getting into the river when we did. The easterly and N.E. winds which prevailed all the time we were at Cape Bathurst continued until the 18th, when it veered round to S.W. by S., and blew a gale; moderated on the evening of the 20th, wind then W. by N., veering round by north; on the 23d was again from the eastward, do., and from the N.E., blowing hard sometimes, until we got into the river. Now, if this gale on the 18th had driven the ice off Cape Bathurst, and we could have got round, we should have been certainly too late to get any distance along the shores of Wollaston Land, even if we had got there at all; and on our return by the way of Bear Lake, come upon Mr. Rae for provision, lost boats and stores, without having done any good.

I hardly know what to say of the position of the lost voyagers, for I cannot think they are shut up in the supposed archipelago S.W. of Cape Walker, and near Wollaston Land, without some of the Hudson's Bay posts hearing of them; for among so many, and Sir J. Franklin knowing the coast so well, some would be ready to undertake the journey, for the distance cannot be very much more than 500 miles to the nearest post, which is Fort Norman. Even could they once get to Bear Lake, Indians might be found ready to assist them. Again, Esquimaux about the Coppermine, and the coast in its vicinity, hunt on Wollaston Land, and surely, if they had been near about them, or found any traces, Sir J. Richardson and Mr. Rae would have heard of it. I am strongly inclined to think, that after visiting Cape Walker, and not finding the route practicable, they have left memorials, pushed through Wellington Channel, thence westward, and are now shut up, far from land, between Melville Island and Point Barrow. My reason for this is, that Captain Fitzjames has so confidently expressed his opinion of that being the direction to be pursued, a route I think impossible to be accomplished; but if the passage is ever to be made, it will be along shore, and only with vessels not exceeding eight feet draft, less, if possible, would be better. Cape Walker, as well as every other likely place for making deposits of their proceedings, ought to be visited at all events.

I was very confident (at least as far as a man can be from circumstances) on starting for this last trip of being able to go from Cape Bathurst to Banks Land; a thought of its impracticability never entered my mind, but I now consider it an undertaking more than boats can effect, in an ice-encumbered sea, with no certainty of falling on intervening land, for in such cases they ought not to be far off shore. People may talk as they like about there being no swell in these seas, but I have seen quite sufficient to overwhelm any such boat that have yet been employed, and have often been detained in consequence. The ice, too, I have seen in such motion, with even a moderate breeze, as to render the position of any boat dangerous that might be among it; I can only compare it (so to speak) to floating rocks, which would go through a boat like a sheet of brown paper, for, smart as you may be, you cannot always get out of its way.

The expeditions out now appear to be better adapted to ensure success than the former ones, both from their size and nature; for steam in these seas has great advantage over sailing vessels, therefore the more fitted for it. May God in His great mercy grant them His aid, and bring all home again to their native land!

On the 21st of October the ice was driving fast from the Liard, on the 26th it was driving from the upper part of the M'Kenzie, and on the 1st of December all was entirely closed up. This was later than it was last year by four days, but the cold did not commence so early then, or was there so much snow on the ground, when the river set fast. There appears to have been no Indian summer this year.

On the 20th of October Mr. Miles, one of the clerks, arrived from the Big Island fishery. This gentleman we found here on our arrival, and accompanied the men to the fishery; he informed me that they had a long and tedious passage up, from the snow lying so deep (making the track-

149

ing heavy) and the quantity of ice they had met along shore; they had been ten days on the voyage, the usual time being only six. His accounts of the fishery was not encouraging, and at a later period, when they met with some success, it was impossible to get the fish down to this post, so that they are very short of the usual supply.

In the beginning of December I heard from the steersman, who informed me, that not only themselves but the Company's people had been badly off for provision lately, the lake freezing and opening again so constantly that it was impossible to set their nets. He had already lost one net, and had been obliged to get two more pieces of pemmican from store; they were in better hopes now, as the lake had at last set fast.[14]

Chapter Five

Fort Simpson to York Factory
and to England
January to October 1851

Commander Pullen and his party spent a long, cold and dreary winter at Fort Simpson and on Big Island. Throughout this period Lieutenant Hooper took a series of meteorological and astronomical observations, and recorded the magnetic dip daily.[1] In these duties he was assisted by Commander Pullen. The first spring thaws took place in April and, by 14 May, ploughing had started at Fort Simpson. The ice began to move in the Liard River on 4 May, and three days later the river in the vicinity of the fort was clear.

On 24 May, Mr. Bell, who was in charge at Fort Simpson, set off down the Mackenzie to Forts Norman and Good Hope, to collect the furs for the spring brigade. Pullen and his men, most of whom had arrived from Big Island, were busy preparing for their long journey across Canada to York Factory. It is not clear if they used the *Try Again* for this purpose, but it seems more than likely. In any case, whatever boat they were to use, was thoroughly refitted, and all stores and equipment no longer required were returned to the Company.

Pullen decided to make an early start and move on slowly, rather than wait for the Mackenzie River Brigade. On the afternoon of 5 June 1851, he and his men left Fort Simpson for the last time, homeward bound for England. They had all been away for over three years, much of the time in open boats north of the Arctic Circle, living and travelling under conditions of considerable danger and discomfort.

153

On 13 June, they arrived at Big Island, where Jerome St. George (*dit* Laporte) was discharged. Ice was met in Great Slave Lake, and it was not until the 20th. that Fort Resolution was reached. Here they were welcomed by Mr. W. McMurray, who was in charge. Pullen waited until 30 June for the Mackenzie River Brigade, and then moved on, up the Slave River to the Noyé Portage (The Portage of the Drowned),[2] which he reached on 9 July. Here he and his men moved all their stores, etc., across the portage, but had to wait for help in moving their boat. On the morning of 10 July, the first group of boats, in charge of Mr. O'Brien, arrived. The boats were soon across this portage which was followed by the Pelican, Mountain and Brûlé Portages. The next day the Embarras and Casette Portages were passed. It was at the latter one that the bottoms of the boats were "burnt" or singed, to get rid of the many splinters that had been acquired, holes and cracks caulked with soft resin, and the bottoms rubbed down with grease.[3] By the afternoon of the 14th. they had entered Lake Athabasca and reached Fort Chipewyan, where Mr. Todd was in charge. Here the brigade rested, though Pullen states that the "inordinate fondness for dancing which all peoples of the country seem possessed of" meant that many of the men left as weary as when they arrived.

On 16 July the brigade moved on, and proceeded by the Embarras River into the Athabasca. Two days later they passed the "pitch springs", the Athabasca tar sands of the present day. The mouth of the Clearwater River was reached on the 21st., and here they spent the night, moving on the following day. On the 24th., they crossed the Cascade and Bonne Portages, horses being hired from the Indians, to transport the cargo and stores at the latter place. The next day the Bigstone, Pine and Terre Blanc Portages were passed, and on 26 July the Mackenzie River Brigade arrived at Portage La Loche (Methy Portage). This was the transfer point between the Mackenzie and Portage La Loche Brigades. The portage was about ten to twelve miles long and crossed the height of land. The rivers on the north side ran eventually into the Beaufort Sea; on the south side into

Hudson's Bay and the Great Lakes. Horses were used to transfer the cargo between the two brigades. Pullen and his men cleared the *Try Again* of all their gear, said good-bye to their trusty and well travelled York Boat, and handed her over to Mr. Bell.

The Portage La Loche Brigade,[4] under the charge of Mr. Alexis L'Esperance,[5] left the Methy Portage on 30 July, and by the following day had crossed Buffalo Lake. They reached Ile à la Crosse Lake on 1 August, and from there until they arrived at Cumberland House on the 13th. life was one steady succession of rapids and portages.[6] The next day they arrived at The Pas, where they were welcomed by the Rev. James Hunter, the Rector of Christ Church, who provided them with eggs, bread and vegetables, a most acceptable change in diet. The church had been started in 1847 and was completed in 1850. During the winter of 1847-48, three of the Sappers and Miners of Sir John Richardson's expedition, went to The Pas to help in the building and furnishing of the church. Two of them were Robert Mackie and James McLaren, Second Corporals, and carpenters by trade. It is known that they built several chairs, some large chests of drawers, the font, pulpit, lectern and the communion rail. Many of these items are still in use at The Pas.

From The Pas, the route led down the Saskatchewan River, through Muddy, Cedar and Cross Lakes, and the Grand Rapid into Lake Winnipeg. The Grand Rapid was swift, deep and turbulent, and was run in twenty-five minutes. It must have been a welcome relief and a most exhilarating experience after so much portaging and back-breaking labour.

On 18 August, the brigade reached Norway House, where Mr. Ross was in charge. Two days later, after many portages, they arrived at Oxford House. On the 27th., the brigade entered the Hay River, and the following morning arrived at York Factory, where Mr. J. Hargrave made Commander Pullen and his men welcome. Here at last was the sea, and lying at anchor off the settlement was the Hudson's Bay Company's barque *Prince of Wales*,[7] Mr. D. Herd, Master.

Pullen and his party embarked in this vessel on 7 September, and two days later sailed for England. The *Prince of Wales* had a good passage across Hudson's Bay and out through the strait, which she cleared on the 18th. Once past Resolution Island and Cape Chidley, she was out into the North Atlantic, passed south of Cape Farewell, homeward-bound for England.

As mentioned on page 94, Commander Pullen rewrote his report of the second expedition which he carried out in 1850. This he delivered to the Admiralty on his arrival in London on 3 October 1851. The second part of this more detailed account, covering the period from January to October 1851, follows:

On the latter end of January 1850 [1851] an express arrived from the northern posts Good Hope and M'Pherson. The river closed up unusually early at Fort M'Pherson on the Peel; all was fast on the 29th of September, and at Fort Good Hope the thermometer in December was down to 50° below zero; cold weather that!

In March I received a letter from Mr. Rae at Fort Confidence, who says, on one occasion the thermometer was down to 72° below zero; so that those of Captain Austin's squadron[8] who have never experienced an Arctic winter will have a good introduction, as I suppose we may fairly conclude that they, being so much further north, will have equally severe cold. Mr. Rae says it was fortunate I did not winter at Fort Franklin, (as was my intention on leaving him,) as the fish there this winter are very scarce, and the poor Indians in the vicinity are actually starving. He appears to have had hard work himself to feed his men, for at the date of his letter, 17th of February, they were all on short allowance.

April 4th, 1851. — The Indians in this vicinity appear to be better off than they were last winter, for as yet only one family have come in starving; that was in February. Rabbits are coming in season again, for we have had them frequently at our table; and for some days last month the dog trains were continually going, bringing in deer meat the hunters had killed. On the 30th one came in and announced that he had no less than fourteen deer in cache; and on 1st April four trains started off to bring them in, and in consequence of the heavy thaws experienced great difficulty in accomplishing their task.

The time appears to be fast approaching, and all are looking forward anxiously for the breaking up of the ice, or some change in the monotonous and dreary landscape around us. I can truly say that in the whole course of my existence I have never wished for time to go by quickly so earnestly; truly the life of a fur trader is not one I should choose. It is now April, and although there has been so many heavy thaws, the season does not appear to be so far advanced as one might expect, or as the last year, for the fine spells have always been followed by severe frost, so that the ground for agricultural purposes is far from being fit for the plough. On the 19th of April we saw the first wild fowl, but cold coming on again they did not remain, it appearing as if they were only the avant couriers of the larger bodies which afterwards passed; many were shot, making an agreeable change in our fare. Ploughing commenced on the 14th of May, and it was well on for the middle of June before all the crops were fairly in the ground. They consisted of barley, potatoes, turnips, and oats for the first time. Last year the ploughing commenced on the 6th of May, and in the first week in June both barley and potatoes were showing above ground.

On the 4th of May the ice from the River Liard made a start three days earlier than it did last year, this time rising higher when moving, and stopping alternately until the 7th; it made a vigorous rush, and soon, from about three miles above Fort Simpson and all down the Mackenzie as far as we could see, was a clear and open channel.

On the 13th May, Mr. Lane, one of the Company's clerks sent in to take charge of Fort Liard, went off for that post; and as the boat was to return I took advantage of the opportunity, and sent Mr. Hooper to obtain the position of the place. On the evening of the 17th the ice from the upper part of the Mackenzie broke up, and came down with a rush; it continued passing in various quantities until the 28th. On the 24th, Chief-trader Bell went off to the northern posts, Forts Norman and Good Hope, to bring their contingent of furs and provisions, the former to go out with the spring brigade. On the evening of the 27th three of the Company's men arrived from Big Island, having left there on the ice on the 30th of April. On their way down the ice broke up, which detained them until the last few days, when the river becoming clear of drifting ice they were enabled to proceed by canoes. From them I heard of our own party; both fish and meat had been very scarce lately (in April), and the men on several occasions were obliged to barter their clothes with the Indians for a meal.

On the 31st of May Mr. Hooper returned; and on the same evening seven of the men arrived from the Slave Lake fishery, so I hope to be able to make an early start for that country we are all anxiously longing to reach.

The observations Mr. Hooper obtained at "Fort des Leards" place it in 60° 13′ 28″ N., and longitude 123° 29′ 42″ W.

The carpenter now commenced on the boat, making good the damages she had received on the coast, while the men were refitting the sails, and handing over all articles to the Company which were not necessary for the voyage through the country, when, on the morning of the 5th June, all was ready to proceed. This was early certainly, but as the river was apparently perfectly free of ice, and I had nothing to detain me longer, rather than wait for the company's boats, which would not start until the 20th, I determined on moving on slowly, and wait for them at the first portage, as we should not be strong enough, unaided, to get our boat over. In the afternoon all about the fort assembled

on the bank to see us off, and we once more bid farewell to
Fort Simpson. Our means of progress, after reaching the
right bank of the river, was, as usual, the tracking line.
When towards evening a breeze sprung up from the westward, and we got on a little faster. The breeze was accompanied with rain, and from this time until we got to Big
Island (the fishing station on the Slave Lake) it hardly ever
ceased. On the 13th we arrived at Big Island, after a passage of eight days; longer than the usual time, certainly, six
being the general average; but we experienced much easterly wind.

Here I discharged one of the company's men (Gerome
Saint George, dit Laport), who had accompanied us to the
coast, and on Monday the 16th moved on to cross the lake
for Fort Resolution. About 10 o'clock we met the ice, which
was lying heavily on the south shores of the lake, extending
far out to the north, and completely barring our progress in
every direction. We pulled into it, in the hopes of being able
to force through; but finding, after struggling with it until 4
p.m., our progress was so slow, that we made for the shore,
steering among some narrow lanes to the westward of the
main body. On nearing the shore we met two canoes containing an Indian family on their way to the eastward, but
had been detained two days by the ice. They were entirely
out of provision, and were waiting patiently for an opportunity to proceed. I gave them some dry meat, which they
attacked, and were soon laughing and chatting away as if
nothing was the matter. We reached the shore at 6 p.m.,
and found the boat had received some slight injury, for she
was making more water than usual; but as there was no
place to haul up we were obliged to keep constantly bailing.
On Tuesday morning, the 17th, the wind was light from the
N.E., when we pulled eastward to a gravelly beach, where
the ice appeared clear; and on landing we were enabled to
haul our boat up for repair. It was done soon; and as there
was no appearance of being able to proceed we all lay down

to sleep. About 10, there was decidedly a change in the ice, affected apparently by the light N.E. wind which had been for some hours blowing, when we again embarked, pulled for the most open part, and after a great deal of pushing managed to get through into a narrow lane of open water leading along shore. The next day we got clear of the ice entirely, and on the morning of the 20th reached Fort Resolution.

As our steersman was not acquainted with the Slave River or any of the rapids, I determined on waiting for the first brigade of boats; but finding on Monday the 30th they did not arrive, I went on, hoping that by a slow progress they would soon catch us up.

Monday 7th. — We reached Salt River, stopped for a day, and on the evening of the 9th reached the first portage. I could not judge for myself of the possibility of our going up the rapids, without other knowledge than that possessed by our steersman, which I saw was wanting; and as none of our men had ever been employed in such work before, nor did I consider we were strong enough to haul the boat up the rapids (even if we knew it) or over the portages, I encamped, unloaded the boat, and carried all the cargo across, to be in readiness for the first brigade. Throughout this day we have had easterly winds, with occasional showers of rain; but in the evening it fell calm, with a heavy down pour, and squalls at times from the westward.

Thursday, July 10th. — About 6 this morning we were awoke up by loud shouting, and on going out saw the first brigade of boats coming up under sail with a strong N. westerly breeze. At half past 6 the first boat landed, and Mr. O'Brien (who was in charge) handed me a letter from Mr. Bell, informing me that Marsellaies, the steersman of the first boat, was an excellent guide for all the rapids, and would take us up. My attention was now directed entirely to the passage, and as I had never been up a rapid before I resolved on going in the first boats, instead of walking across the portage. As soon as Marsellaies' boat was ready, we, in their company, shoved off, pulled across an inshore rapid, and on arriving at the foot of the one we were to go up the two crews disembarked, got the main tracking line on the first boat, and much sooner than I expected got her up the rapid. All then returned for the second (ours,) and she was hauled up in like manner, and with like success.

This rapid is called the Noyé (or drowned rapid), formed by the strong current rushing over a very uneven and rocky bottom, on rather an inclined plane. There are several low rocky islands here in the river, forming many channels; but the one we took is, I believe, the only one the company's boats use, either in passing up or down. To an experienced person it would be difficult to decide on which channel to take, and to a new hand rather appalling; but as Marseillaies appeared to be perfectly competent, and was strongly recommended, I felt every confidence, and, notwithstanding the roaring and boiling of the angry stream, I felt the boat was perfectly safe as long as our line held on.

The portage is on the right bank of the river, about a quarter of a mile in length. When as soon as we had got the boats to its S.E. end, and loaded again for starting, the second brigade of boats arrived at the lower end of the fall. Mr. Bell was in charge; and from Mr. Ross, who accompanied him, I learnt that he had letters for me from Mr. Rae, but as we were ready to proceed I did not wait for them. The next portage was the Pelican, where the rapid was much stronger and more difficult; however, we got over it safely, but not without shipping some water, the following boats preferring hauling over the land than attempting it. From this we soon reached the Mountain, which in fact is a fall of 10 feet; but the portage is a narrow strip of high rock, over which we were obliged to haul the boat before we could again proceed. Next followed the Brule, of about 300 yards in length, over which, after unlading, the boats were to be launched; but it was late when we reached it, there-

161

fore the cargoes were only transported, and we encamped at the upper end of it and on the right bank of the river. Weather during the day showery, with squalls of wind from N.N.W.

Friday, 11th. — This morning early the boats were hauled over the portage, which occupied the people at least an hour and a half, when we again embarked, and during the day successively passed the Embarras, Island, and Casette rapids, the second of which was only a narrow and swift run of water, where we had partially to unload the boats, and haul up with the main line.

The Embarras is a narrow and short rapid, but entirely stopped up with drift wood. Hence the necessity of hauling the boats over the land. At the upper end of the Casette we encamped, as the boats were very much rubbed and splintered in hauling over the portages, and required burning. Here we were joined by the other boats of both brigades, all encamping together for the night.

Saturday, 12th. — At 4 this morning we moved on, passing through a very narrow channel, when we soon got into the main river, and at 7 in the evening stopped for the night on the left bank of the river. At 9.35 a lunar eclipse commenced, and soon after I saw to the westward, although very light, a splendid meteor or star fall, when almost immediately Mr. Hooper saw to the N.W. by W. (compass) another more brilliant, which was directly succeeded, and from where the latter fell, by a faint light, or a large star with a comet-like tail; above it, or from the star, was a very narrow serpentine train of light very much resembling a thread of small beads. A dark night would have shown it more distinctly; its elevation was about 20°, and was visible for about half an hour. The next night I looked for it again, but not seeing anything, although several stars were visible, concluded it was nothing more than a meteor or fire ball. It looked like this:

The weather is now intensely hot, the thermometer at noon standing at 104° in the sun, and under a black hand-kerchief as high as 112°; this, with the accompaniment of mosquitoes, is not very pleasant, or do we get much rest during the night.

At 5.30, on the morning of the 14th, we entered the "River de Rocher" (which leads into the Athabasca Lake), at the junction of the Slave and Peace Rivers; and about 3 p.m. entered the Athabasca Lake, steering eastward through an archipelago of islands; at 5 we landed at Fort Chipewayan.

At this post we remained all the next day, for the express purpose of giving the men a rest, but from the inordinate fondness for dancing which all the people of the country seem possessed of, it is greatly neutralized, for when they once begin there is no knowing when they will leave off, and many of the men showed consequence of it on again embarking.

This station is the largest of the company's establishments we have yet seen; is situated on an island, its south point, and on a very rocky foundation. From it you have a most delightful view of the lake, which is studded with islands, well earning its Indian name of Lake of the Hills, from their hilly appearance. The soil about the fort is rocky, but on the lower land is light and sandy, where I saw some potatoes growing. On another island (where now are the ruins of a station occupied in the days of the two companies) is a good garden, with other vegetables besides potatoes.

Wednesday, 16th. — Mr. Bell, with three boats, went off early this morning, and as I was not so anxious about leaving, or wishing rather to give my men as much rest as possible, for they really have heavy work, and in a broiling hot sun, with the mosquitoes so troublesome at night that it is almost impossible to get any sleep, I did not think of leaving until after breakfast. Having to provide provision for a longer period than would occupy as to the portage "La Loche" (on Methy Portage), I took from this three bags of pemmican; and at 11, with five other boats, shoved off. Four of these were of the second brigade, the fifth was of the first, but Marsellaie steered her, and as we required his services in the rapids, he of course kept with us. We left with a fair wind, which soon carried us across the lake to the entrance of a narrow and long channel, called the "Embarras," which would considerably lessen our distance to the Athabasca River, than if we were obliged to round the more easterly islands. The entrance of this channel was rather difficult of access from shoalwater, which we heard at the fort was extraordinarily so, but with a little management and good pilotage we got snugly into it, made a good day's progress, and the next day in the afternoon, Thursday the 17th, got into the Athabasca River.

The "Embarras" in no place exceeds 100 yards in breadth, and with a slack current, makes it preferable as a route to the main river, where the current is very strong. Its banks in places are steep, and, like the Slave River, thickly clothed with willow and poplar, some of the latter very large. The waters are abominably dirty, so that we get a pretty good share of mud in our drink, never allowing it sufficient time to settle.

Friday, 18th. — It was 4 this morning before we moved on, 3 or half past 2 previously having been the general time. The weather still continues very hot, with our particular friends, mosquitoes, as troublesome as ever. With any thing of a breeze, Marsellaies' boat and ours generally ran away from the others, and to-day, as we have been favoured, made the most of it, leaving the others far astern, and did not see them again until the morning of the 20th, when we stopped to cut up a deer one of the Indians had shot when in the act of crossing the river. This was a most acceptable prize, particularly as the pemmican last opened, which was received at Fort Chippewaw, was not good; in fact unfit for use. A small portion of our prize was given to the second brigade. When after breakfast we again proceeded. In the afternoon we stopped at the pitch springs; filled up the casks; again moved on until half past seven, when we encamped for the night, and were soon joined by the second brigade of boats.

These pitch springs issue from the face of a hill (on the right bank of the River Athabasca), and about a couple of hundred yards from the water. There are several others in the river; but it is from these the company get their supplies for the use of boats, etc. They occupy a space on the surface of about nine feet square. From the upper or higher part, the pitch issues clear and pure in a narrow stream, mixing up at the bottom or lower part with mud and sand in a thick mass, which is what the kegs are filled with, and purified by boiling.

At a quarter after 5 of the afternoon of the 21st we reached the junction of the Clear Water River with the Athabasca, turned into the former, and encamped at its mouth.

On the afternoon of the 24th we reached the Cascade Portage. Here the boats were cleared of every thing and taken up the rapid, which was very shallow, consequently taking a long time to perform the service. The men then had to return and carry the goods, so that it was late before we reached the next portage (the Bonne). This portage is the longest we have yet had, being about 1 1/4 mile over; but finding here several Indians encamped, with horses for hire, I secured a number for taking the things of the party over. The boats were now perfectly light. However, from the rapid being very shallow and long, it was almost dark before they got the boat up, and encamped for the night. About 1 this afternoon we were joined by two men from the Portage "La Loche" brigade. They informed us provisions were very short at the portage, and that Isle à la Crosse, the first post on the route after leaving it, was deficient of any supplies. This was not very encouraging, for the provisions of my party was nearly exhausted.

25th July. — This morning we moved on about the usual time, and in something less than an hour reached the Big-stone Portage, a short one, where only the goods were to be carried, the boats going up the rapid by line. The next was the Pine Portage; rather a longer one, but passed in the same manner as the last. When at 7 p.m. we reached the Terre Blank, or white mud, which is the last before reaching the long Portage "La Loche." Here we were obliged to take every thing across, boats as well as goods, which took us quite until dark before the job was accomplished. However, the boats were loaded again, to be ready for an early start the next morning. The Terre Blank is a succession of falls passing between steep precipices, from which we got a view, as well as a good wetting from the long damp grass.

The second brigade arrived before we had completed the transit of our boats.

26th July. — Started at 4 this morning, and at noon reached the long-desired Portage "La Loche" (or Methey), and received from Mr. Ross (who had preceded us) a parcel of letters from dear home, which had been long most anxiously looked for. Here I learnt that a canoe was on the route from Montreal with letters, and from the Red River three boats with provisions for the expedition.

Many were the conjectures respecting these boats, fancying they might be conveying orders to me for a further search, and that we might again be destined to another grievous disappointment. However, there was no help for it.

Our boat was now cleared of every thing; and she had all her stores handed over to Mr. Bell, and our things prepared for transportation to the other end of the portage to-morrow. L'Esperance, the person in charge of the brigade there, had arrived four days ago, and nearly completed the discharge and transport of his cargoes to the middle of the portage. During the evening and great part of the night much rain fell; a common occurrence here at this season.

27th July. — Part of our goods were taken over the portage this day on horses, the men accompanying them, Mr. Hooper and self also, and we reached the eastern end, where L'Esperance was encamped, about 6 p.m. Midway, I found all the goods for the Mackenzie River district which L'Esperance had brought in with his brigade. As we were so short of provision, I took a bag of flour for the party.

Portage "La Loche" is the longest of any, and called by the company's people 11 or 12 miles, but I do not think it so much; nine, I should say, was the longest. After ascending a steep hill on the Clear Water River side, the road gradually descends to the eastward to "Lac la Loche," passing through a thickly wooded country, over a light sandy soil. In fact it is the height of land; all waters running north of it running to the Arctic Ocean; south to the Atlantic.

30th July. — This morning L'Esperance commenced the lading of his brigade of five boats, and as I intended accompanying him, the men were divided among them. When at 11 we proceeded; and on the 1st of August, at 2 p.m., reached "Isle à la Crosse." As provisions were here very scarce, I got a bullock, which was immediately slaughtered, divided amongst the boats, and we again started.

On the morning of the 7th of August we met the Athabasca brigade of four boats, and landed with them to get the news. Messrs. Dechambeau and Boucher were in charge, with Mrs. and Miss Lane passengers. From them we heard that Mr. Anderson was close at hand, with the

167

three boats we had been so anxiously looking for. After half an hour we moved on again, and in a short time fell in with Mr. Anderson with four boats, stopping at the old fort of the Rapid River. We pulled across to them (as we were keeping the opposite shore); landed, and breakfasted all together. From Mr. Anderson, who is going in to take charge of the Mackenzie River district, I learnt that three of his boats were laden with flour and pemmican, to be placed in depot at the several posts in the Mackenzie District likely to be visited by any of the searched for or searching parties, improbable as the former appears to be. Mr. Anderson also told me that Manuel, the man who acted so conspicuous a part in the massacre of the Esquimaux at Point Separation, has been ordered to Canada for trial.

At 8.40 we again proceeded; and at 8 a.m. on the 18th of August arrived at Norway House. Here we remained until 6 in the evening, when L'Esperance shoved off. Arrived at Oxford House early on the morning of the 23d, and at York Factory the morning of the 28th. The Hudson's Bay Company's ship was lying in the roads. We embarked on the 7th of September, sailed on the 9th, and on the 4th of October the ship entered the East India Docks, and my men were removed to H.M. Ship "Crocodile" off the Tower. [9]

W. J. S. Pullen, Commander R.N.

At 7.15 a.m., 2 October 1851, the *Prince of Wales* passed Dungeness, and shortly thereafter the Dover pilot cutter put Mr. T. Austin, Pilot, on board. At the same time Commander Pullen, Lieutenant Hooper and Mr. O'Brien of the Hudson's Bay Company went ashore in the lugger *Prince of Wales*, and were landed at Deal. Pullen went straight up to London, and on 3 October wrote to the Admiralty.

Ship Hotel Charing Cross,
3rd October 1851.

Sir,

I have the honour to report to you for the information of their Lordships of the Admiralty my arrival in England. I left Fort Simpson on the 5th of June 1851 and reached York Factory on the 28th of August. On the 7th September we embarked in the Hudson's Bay Company Ship *Prince of Wales.* Sailed on the 9th., cleared Hudson's Bay and Straight under most favourable circumstances on the 18th., and yesterday passed through the Downs. I landed at Deal and made the best of my way to London, and beg that their Lordships will be pleased to inform me where my men are to be placed.

The ship it is likely will reach the East India Docks tomorrow, when I hope shortly to lay before their Lordships my journal of my last trip on the coast in full detail, together with such observations as I have been able to make. In conclusion I am happy to state that Mr. Hooper's exertions in the service I have been engaged on has been most praiseworthy, as well as that of my boats crews, whose names I herewith enclose.

I have the honour to be,
Sir,
Your obedient servant.
W.J.S. Pullen.

John Hemmett,
    Sailmaker.
Wm. Salmon,
    Capts. Coxswain.
Jas. Whaby, A.B.
Thos. Mellish, A.B.
Wm. Seymour, A.B.

John Robinson, A.B.
Jas. Tullock, A.B.
Wm. McCarthy, A.B.
R. Tullock
    Royal Marines.
J. Herd,
    Royal Marines.[10]

The *Prince of Wales* arrived at the East India Docks on the afternoon of 3 October, the seamen and marines being discharged to H.M.S. *Crocodile*, the receiving ship lying off the Tower. Pullen's last letter dealing with his boat expedition, was written on 20 October 1851.

16 Buckingham Street, Adelphi,
October 20th., 1851.

Sir,

    As I have now handed in my journals in full detail of my last trip to the Arctic Coast, in addition to the former one, in search of the missing voyagers, and tho' I have been unfortunately unsuccessful yet I hope that their Lordships are satisfied with our exertions to carry out their orders, and although we were a small party I trust their Lordships will not consider us unworthy of their approbation.

    In reference to either of my journals I think their Lordships will perceive that we have not been without our share of hardship and privation; and that with the slightest possibility of doing we have never been inactive, nor shrunk from any dangers or difficulty that we have met with.

I have the honour to be,
Sir,
Your obedient servant,
W.J.S. Pullen.
The Secretary of the Admiralty, London.[11]

This was the termination of three and a half years of great endeavour, immense hardship and privation, considerable risk and much travelling, all in the search of Sir John Franklin and his expedition. In all this, Pullen was not successful, but at least he established the fact that there was no trace of Franklin west of Cape Bathurst. Commander Pullen, Lieutenant Hooper with the ten seamen and two marines, had contributed their share to the opening of the Arctic frontier of Canada, and in doing so had demonstrated the ability of British seamen to face and overcome any hardship, and do so with cheerfulness and fortitude.

The Admiralty replied to Commander Pullen's letter of 20 October the following day.

Admiralty, 21st October 1851.

Sir,

Having received and laid before my Lords Commissioners of the Admiralty your letter of the 20th instant, I am commanded by their Lordships to convey to you their approval of your services and conduct during the overland expedition on which you have been employed, an approval which my Lords have much satisfaction in conveying to you; and you are also to express to Lieutenant Hooper, and the men under your command, their Lordships satisfaction at having received reports of their perseverance and good conduct in the performance of the above service.

I am, etc.,
J. Parker.[12]

In December 1851, Commander Pullen put forward a search plan which suggested the use of a small steam vessel. The following January he wrote to the Admiralty offering his services in what was to be known as the Belcher Expedition, the last Admiralty organized search for Franklin. He was appointed to command H.M.S. *North Star* in the rank of Commander, with his brother, T.C. Pullen serving as the Master. Just over six months after returning from a three and a half years of service in the search for Franklin, W.J.S. Pullen was off once more engaged in the same undertaking. The Belcher Expedition sailed from the Thames on 21 April 1852, but that is another story.

171

Notes, Appendices,
Bibliography, and Index

Notes

PROLOGUE

1 *Appendix One.* P.P., Vol. XLI, 1847-48. Paper 264, pp. 3-7.
   Copy of Instructions to Captain Sir John Franklin, K.C.H., Her Majesty's Ship "Erebus", dated 5 May 1845.

2 Baird, P.D. *Expeditions to the Canadian Arctic.*
   The Beaver, March, June and September, 1949, pp. 7-11.

3 *Appendix Two.* P.P. Vol. XLI, 1847-48. Paper 264, pp. 7-12.
   Copy of Instructions addressed to Lieutenant (now Commander) Thomas E.L. Moore, commanding Her Majesty's Brig "Plover", dated 3 January 1848, and further correspondence.
   See Note 20 for the Admiralty's instructions to Captain Kellett of H.M.S. *Herald.*

4 *Appendix Three.* P.P. Vol. XLI, 1847-48. Paper 386.
   A copy of the orders from the Lords Commissioners of the Admiralty under which Captain Sir James Clark Ross, R.N., has proceeded on an expedition in search of Sir John Franklin.

5 P.P. Vol. XLI, 1847-48. Paper 264, pp. 37-40.

6 *Appendix Four.* P.P. Vol. XLI, 1847-48. Paper 264, pp. 19-21.
   Instructions to Sir John Richardson, M.D., 16 March 1848. By the Commissioners for executing the office of Lord High Admiral, etc.

7   Richardson, Sir J. *Arctic Searching Expedition*. New York: Harper and Brothers, 1852, pp. 32-37.

8   P.P. Vol. XLI, 1847-48. Paper 264, pp. 58-73.
    See Appendix Nine for the names of these men.

9   Ibid. p. 73, p. 75.

10 Ibid. pp. 12-16.

11 Ibid. pp. 71-72.

12 Ibid. p. 77.

13 Ibid. p. 76.

14 William John Samuel Pullen, eldest son of Lieutenant William Pullen, R.N., and Amelia Mary, née Haswell, born 4 December 1813. Educated at the Greenwich Hospital School, and joined the Royal Navy as a First Class Volunteer, being appointed to H.M.S. *Britannia* on 15 June 1828. Passed the provisional examination for Second Master on 25 July 1835. Left the Royal Navy in 1836, for service as an assistant surveyor under Colonel Light in South Australia. Returned to England in 1842 and rejoined the Royal Navy. He was appointed to H.M. Steam Surveying Vessel *Columbia*, Captain P.F. Shortland, R.N., surveying in the Bay of Fundy. Promoted to Mate, 20 July 1844, Lieutenant, 9 November 1846, Commander, 25 January 1850, Captain 10 May 1856. See D.N.B., Vol. 66, p. 465.

15 P.P. Vol. XLI, 1847-48. Paper 264, pp. 74-75.

16 Pullen, W.J.S. *Narrative by Vice Admiral W.J.S. Pullen.*
    Public Library, Museum and Art Gallery of South Australia, pp. 11-12.

17 Ibid. p. 12.

18 P.P. Vol. XLI, 1847-48. Paper 264, p. 79.

19 Seemann, B.C. *Narrative of the Voyage of H.M.S. Herald during the years 1845-51, under the command of Captain Henry Kellett, R.N., C.B.*
    London, Reeve & Co. 1853, Vol. I, p. 229.

20 *Appendix Five.* P.P. Vol. XLI, 1847-48. Paper 264, pp. 16-18. *Instructions to Captain Kellett, Her Majesty's Ship "Herald," 13 December 1847.*

21 P.P. Vol. XLI, 1847-48. Paper 264, pp. 81-82.

22 Seemann, B.C. *Narrative of the Voyage of H.M.S. Herald during the years 1845-51, under the command of Captain Henry Kellett, R.N., C.B.* London, Reeve & Co., 1853, Vol. I, p. 229.

23 Hooper, W.H. *Ten Months in the Tents of the Tuski.* London, John Murray, 1853, p. 3.

24 P.P. Vol. XLI, 1847-48. Paper 264, p. 75.

25 P.R.O. Adm. 7/189. *Report of Proceedings of H.M.S. Plover, dated 25 September 1849.*

CHAPTER ONE

1 *Appendix Six.* P.R.O., Adm. 7/189. *Commander T.E.L. Moore's orders to Lieutenant W.J.S. Pullen, commanding the Boat Expedition, dated 25 July 1849.*

2 *Appendix Seven.* P.R.O., Adm. 7/189. *Captain Henry Kellett's instructions to Lieutenant W.J.S. Pullen, commanding the Boat Expedition, dated 25 July 1849.*

3 See Note 1.

4 P.R.O. Adm. 7/189. *Report of Proceedings of H.M.S. Herald, dated 22 November 1849.*

5 P.R.O. Adm. 7/189.

6 Ibid. Adm. 7/189.

7 Baidar. This was probably a umiak, which was an Eskimo skin boat of good carrying capacity. It was known as the "women's boat." See *Canoes and Kayaks of Western America*, Bill Durham, Copper Canoe

Press, Seattle, 1960, pp. 21-22, and *The Bark Canoe and Skin Boats of North America*, Adney and Chapelle, Smithsonian Institution, Washington, 1964, pp. 175-190.

8   P.R.O. Adm. 7/189.

9   Ibid. Adm. 7/189.

10   Ibid. Adm. 7/189. *Report of Proceedings of H.M.S. Herald, dated 22 November 1849.*

11   Franklin, John. *Narrative of a Second Expedition to the Shores of the Polar Sea, in the years 1825, 1826 and 1827.* London, J. Murray, 1828, p. 148.

12   *Appendix Eight.* P.R.O., Adm. 7/189. *Dr. Rae to Sir John Richardson, from Fort Simpson, 5 October 1849.*

13   *Appendix Nine.* P.R.O., Adm. 38/2041. *A list of the officers, seamen and marines who formed the crews of the two 27 foot gig whale-boats.*

14   P.R.O. Adm. 7/189.

15   Ibid. Adm. 7/189. *Report of Proceedings of H.M.S. Herald, dated 22 November 1849.*

16   See Note 11.

17   Bredin, T.F. " 'Whale Island' and the Mackenzie Delta: Charted errors and unmapped discoveries, 1789 to 1850." *Arctic*, Journal of the Arctic Institute of North America, Vol. 15, No. 1, 1962.

18   Smith, D. Murray. *Arctic Discoveries from British and Foreign Shores from the earliest times to the Expedition of 1875-76.* M'Gready, Thompson & Niven, Glasgow, Melbourne and Dunedin, 1877, p. 457.

19   See Note 12.

20   P.R.O. Adm. 7/189.

CHAPTER TWO

[1] P.P. Vol. xxxv, 1850, Paper 107, pp. 58-64. *Narrative of the Proceedings of Captain Sir James C. Ross in Command of the Expedition through Lancaster Sound and Barrow Strait.*

Gilpin, J.D. *Outline of the Voyage of H.M.S. Enterprize and Investigator to Barrow Strait in search of Sir John Franklin, The Nautical Magazine,* London, 1850, pp. 8-19, 82-90, 160-70, 230.

Smith, D. Murray. *Arctic Expeditions from British and Foreign Shores from the earliest times to the Expedition of 1875-76,* pp. 482-484.

[2] H.B.R.S. Vol. xvi, 1953. *Rae's Arctic Correspondence, 1844-55,* pp. 80-85.

Richardson, Sir J. *Arctic searching expedition,* New York, Harper and Brothers, 1852.

[3] *Appendix Four.* P.P., Vol. xli, 1847-48, Paper 264, pp. 19-21. *Instructions to Sir John Richardson, M.D., 16 March 1848. By the Commissioners for executing the office of Lord High Admiral etc.*

[4] H.B.R.S. Vol. xvi, 1953. *Rae's Arctic Correspondence, 1844-55,* pp. 98-100.

[5] Ibid. pp. 1-1ii.

[6] Ibid. pp. 101-102.

[7] Ibid. pp. 103-117.

[8] Ibid. p. 118.

Richardson, Sir J. *Arctic searching expedition,* New York, Harper and Brothers, 1852, pp. 309-315.

[9] See Chapter One, pp. 45-51, 52-68.

[10] Collinson, R. *Journal of H.M.S. Enterprise, on the expedition in search of Sir John Franklin's ships by Behring's Strait, (1850-55).* London; Sampson, Low; 1889.

Armstrong, Alex. *A personal narrative of the discovery of the North-West Passage . . . during nearly five years continuous service in the Arctic Regions while in search of the Arctic expedition under Sir John Franklin*, London; Hurst & Blackett; 1857.

M'Clure, R.J. *The discovery of the North-West Passage by H.M.S. Investigator, Captain R.M. M'Clure, 1850, 1851, 1852, 1853, 1854.* Edited by Commander Sherard Osborn, London, Longmans; 1856.

Miertsching, J. *Frozen Ships. The Arctic Diary of Johann Miertsching, 1850 - 1854.* Translated by L.H. Neatby. Toronto, Macmillan of Canada, 1967.

[11] In 1848/50 the record for the passage from Liverpool to New York was 11 days 3 hours, and New York to Liverpool, 10 days 9 hours. The R.M.S. *Europa* of the British & North American Royal Mail Steam Packet Company of Samuel Cunard, was the record holder both ways.

[12] *Appendix Ten.* P.R.O., Adm. 2/1608. *Admiralty orders of 25 January 1850, to Commander Pullen to continue the search, if he thought it adviseable.*

CHAPTER THREE

[1] Hooper. W.H. *Ten Months among the Tents of the Tuski*, London, John Murray, 1853, p. 269, pp. 277-285.

[2] H.B.R.S. Vol. XVI, 1953. *Rae's Arctic Correspondence, 1844-55*, pp. 364-365.

[3] Hooper, W.H. *Ten Months among the Tents of the Tuski*, London, John Murray, 1853, pp. 299-302.

[4] *Appendix Ten.* P.R.O., Adm. 2/1608. *Admiralty orders of 25 January 1850, to Commander Pullen to continue the search if he thought it adviseable.*

[5] *Appendix Eleven.* P.R.O., Adm. 7/189. *Letter from Lady Franklin to Captain W.A.B. Hamilton, R.N., Second Secretary to the Admiralty, on the promotion of Commander Moore and Lieutenant Pullen.*

[6] *Appendix Twelve.* P.R.O., Adm. 7/191. *Commander Pullen to Dr. Rae, 28 June 1850.*

[7] H.B.R.S. Vol. XVI, 1953. *Rae's Arctic Correspondence*, 1844-55, p. 366.

[8] Ibid. p. 350.

[9] Ibid. p. 357.

[10] Ibid. p. 124.

[11] P.R.O. Adm. 7/191.

[12] Ibid. Adm. 7/191.

CHAPTER FOUR

[1] "York Boats," *The Beaver*, March 1949, pp. 19-23.
See also Appendix Thirteen, p. 223.

[2] Halkett Boat. This was an inflatable india-rubber boat with a canvas cover, invented by Lieutenant Peter Halkett, R.N., in the early 1840s. It was 9′ 6″ long, 4′ 9″ wide, oval in shape, and fitted with a bellows and two paddles. One of these boats was used by Dr. Rae in his expedition of 1846-47, and had carried two men and over 200 lbs. of stores.
Ref: *The Beaver*, Spring 1955, pp. 46-48. *The Mariner's Mirror*, Vol. 44, 1958, pp. 154-158.

[3] H.B.R.S. Vol. XVI, 1953. *Rae's Arctic Correspondence*, 1844-55, p. 124.

[4] Ibid. p. 350, p. 366.

[5] P.R.O. Adm. 7/191.

[6] H.B.R.S. Vol. XVI, 1953. *Rae's Arctic Correspondence*. 1844-55, pp. 141-142.

[7] Bredin, T.F. *"Whale Island" and the Mackenzie Delta: Charted Errors and Unmapped Discoveries, 1789 to 1850*, p. 64.

Mackay, J.R. *The Mackenzie Delta Area, N.W.T.*, pp. 9-10.

[8] P.R.O. Adm. 7/191.

[9] to [13] See Note 2.

[14] P.R.O. Adm. 7/191.

CHAPTER FIVE

[1] Hooper, W.H. *Ten Months among the Tents of the Tuski*. London, John Murray, 1853, p. 376.

[2] Franklin, John. *Narrative of a Journey to the Shores of the Polar Sea in the years 1819-20-21-22*. London, John Murray, 1824, Vol. I, pp. 304-5.

[3] Hooper, W.H. *Ten Months among the Tents of the Tuski*. London, John Murray, 1853, p. 402.

[4] Turner, J.P. "The La Loche Brigade." *The Beaver*, December 1943, pp. 32-36.

[5] Ibid. p. 33.

[6] Hooper, W.H. *Ten Months among the Tents of the Tuski*. London, John Murray, 1853, pp. 409-415.

[7] Cotton, H.M.S. "The ship Prince of Wales." *The Beaver*, March 1934, pp. 42-44.
Prince of Wales, barque 507 tons, 135 ft. x 28 1/2 ft. x 18.3 ft. Registered London. Built by M & D.L. Wigram, Southampton, and launched March 1850. Sold 1885.

8   H.M. Ships *Resolute*, Captain H.T. Austin, R.N. *Assistance*, Captain E. Ommanney, R.N., *Intrepid*, Lieutenant J.B. Cator, R.N., and *Pioneer*, Lieutenant S. Osmer, R.N.

9   P.R.O. Adm. 7/191.

10 Ibid. Adm. 7/191.

11 Ibid. Adm. 7/191.

12 Ibid. Adm. 7/191.

Appendices

APPENDIX ONE

P.P. Vol. XLI, 1847-48. Paper 264, pp 3-7.

Copies of Instructions to Captain Sir John Franklin, in reference to the ARC-TIC EXPEDITION of 1845; and to the Officers who have been appointed to command Expeditions in search of Sir John Franklin.

Copy of Instructions addressed to Captain Sir John Franklin, K.C.H., Her Majesty's Ship "Erebus," dated 5th May 1845, —

By the Commissioners for executing the office of Lord High Admiral of the United Kingdom of Great Britain and Ireland.

1. Her Majesty's Government having deemed it expedient that a further attempt should be made for the accomplishment of a northwest passage by sea from the Atlantic to the Pacific Ocean, of which passage a small portion only remains to be completed, we have thought proper to appoint you to the command of the expedition to be fitted out for that service, consisting of Her Majesty's Ships "Erebus," and "Terror;" and you are hereby required and directed, so soon as the said ships shall be in all respects ready for sea, to proceed forthwith in the "Erebus" under your command, taking with you Her Majesty's ship "Terror," her Captain (Crozier), having been placed by us under your orders, taking also with you the "Barretto Junior" transport, which has been directed to be put at your disposal for the purpose of carrying out portions of your provisions, clothing, and other stores.

2. On putting to sea, you are to proceed, in the first place, by such a route as, from the wind and weather, you may deem to be the most suitable for despatch, to Davis' Strait, taking the transport with you to such a distance up that Strait as you may be able to proceed without impediment from ice, being careful not to risk that vessel by allowing her to be beset in the ice, or exposed to any violent contact with it; you will then avail yourself of the earliest opportunity of clearing the transport of the provisions and stores with which she is charged for the use of the expedition, and you are then to send her back to England, giving to the agent or master such directions for his guidance as may appear to you most proper, and reporting by that opportunity your proceedings to our secretary, for our information.

3. You will then proceed in the execution of your orders into Baffin's Bay, and get as soon as possible to the western side of the Strait, provided it should appear to you that the ice chiefly prevails on the eastern side, or near the middle; the object being to enter Lancaster Sound with as little delay as possible; but as no specific directions can be given, owing to the position of the ice varying from year to year, you will, of course, be guided by your own observations as to the course most eligible to be taken, in order to ensure a speedy arrival in the Sound above mentioned.

4. As, however, we have thought fit to cause each ship to be fitted with a small steam-engine and propellor, to be used only in pushing the ships through channels between masses of ice, when the wind is adverse, or in a calm, we trust the difficulty usually found in such cases will be much obviated, but as the supply of fuel to be taken in the ships is necessarily small, you will use it only in cases of difficulty.

5. Lancaster Sound, and its continuation through Barrow's Strait, having been four times navigated without any impediment by Sir Edward Parry, and since frequently by whaling ships, will probably be found without any obstacles from ice or islands; and Sir Edward Parry having also proceeded from the latter in a straight course to Melville Island, and returned without experiencing any, or very little, difficulty, it is hoped that the remaining portion of the passage, about 900 miles, to Bhering's Strait may also be found equally free from obstruction; and in proceeding to the westward, therefore, you will not stop to examine any openings either to the

northward or southward in that Strait, but continue to push to the westward without loss of time, in the latitude of about 74°, till you have reached the longitude of that portion of land on which Cape Walker is situated, or about 98° west. From that point we desire that every effort be used to endeavour to penetrate to the south-ward and westward in a course as direct towards Bhering's Strait as the position and extent of the ice, or the existence of land, at present unknown, may admit.

6. We direct you to this particular part of the Polar Sea as affording the best prospect of accomplishing the passage to the Pacific, in consequence of the unusual magnitude and apparently fixed state of the barrier of ice observed by the "Hecla" and "Griper," in the year 1820, off Cape Dundas, the south-western extremity of Mel-ville Island; and we, therefore, consider that loss of time would be incurred in renewing the attempt in that direction; but should your progress in the direction before ordered be arrested by ice of a permanent appearance, and that when passing the mouth of the Strait, between Devon and Cornwallis Islands, you had observed that it was open and clear of ice; we desire that you will duly con-sider, with reference to the time already consumed, as well as to the symptoms of a late or early close of the season, whether that channel might not offer a more practicable outlet from the Archi-pelago, and a more ready access to the open sea, where there would be neither islands nor banks to arrest and fix the floating masses of ice; and if you should have advanced too far to the south-westward to render it expedient to adopt this new course before the end of the present season, and if, therefore, you should have determined to winter in that neighbourhood, it will be a mat-ter for your mature deliberation whether in the ensuing season you would proceed by the above-mentioned Strait, or whether you would persevere to the south-westward, according to the former directions.

7. You are well aware, having yourself been one of the intelligent tra-vellers who have traversed the American shore of the Polar Sea, that the groups of islands that stretch from that shore to the north-ward to a distance not yet known, do not extend to the westward further than about the 120th degree of western longitude, and that beyond this, and to Bhering's Strait, no land is visible from the American shore of the Polar Sea.

8. Should you be so fortunate as to accomplish a passage through Bhering's Strait, you are then to proceed to the Sandwich Islands, to refit the ships and refresh the crews, and if, during your stay at such place, a safe opportunity should occur of sending one of your officers or despatches to England by Panama, you are to avail yourself of such opportunity to forward to us as full a detail of your proceedings and discoveries as the nature of the conveyance may admit of, and in the event of no such opportunity offering during your stay at the Sandwich Islands, you are on quitting them to proceed with the two ships under your command off Panama, there to land an officer with such despatches, directing him to make the best of his way to England with them, in such a manner as our Consul at Panama shall advise, after which you are to lose no time in returning to England by way of Cape Horn.

9. If at any period of your voyage the season shall be so far advanced as to make it unsafe to navigate the ships, and the health of your crews, the state of the ships, and all concurrent circumstances should combine to induce you to form the resolution of wintering in those regions, you are to use your best endeavours to discover a sheltered and safe harbour, where the ships may be placed in security for the winter, taking such measures for the health and comfort of the people committed to your charge as the materials with which you are provided for housing in the ships, may enable you to do – and if you should find it expedient to resort to this measure, and you should meet with any inhabitants, either Esquimaux or Indians, near the place where you winter, you are to endeavour by every means in your power to cultivate a friendship with them, by making them presents of such articles as you may be supplied with, and which may be useful or agreeable to them; you will, however, take care not to suffer yourself to be surprized by them but use every precaution, and be constantly on your guard against any hostility: you will, by offering rewards, to be paid in such manner as you may think best, prevail on them to carry to any of the settlements of the Hudson's Bay Company, an account of your situation and proceedings, with an urgent request that it may be forwarded to England with the utmost possible despatch.

10. In an undertaking of this description, much must be always left to the discretion of the commanding officer, and, as the objects of this Expedition have been fully explained to you, and you have already had much experience on service of this nature, we are con-

vinced we cannot do better than leave it to your judgement, in the event of your not making a passage this season, either to winter on the coast, with the view of following up next season any hopes or expectations which your observations this year may lead you to entertain, or to return to England to report to us the result of such observations, always recollecting our anxiety for the health, comfort and safety of yourself, your officers and men; and you will duly weigh how far the advantage of starting next season from an advanced position may be counterbalanced by what may be suffered during the winter, and by the want of such refreshment and refitting as would be afforded by your return to England.

11. We deem it right to caution you against suffering the two vessels placed under your orders to separate, except in the event of accident or unavoidable necessity, and we desire you to keep up the most unreserved communications with the commander of the "Terror," placing in him every proper confidence, and acquainting him with the general tenor of your orders, and with your views and intentions from time to time in the execution of them, that the service may have the full benefit of your united efforts in the prosecution of such a service; and that, in the event of unavoidable separation, or of any accident to yourself, Captain Crozier may have the advantage of knowing, up to the latest practicable period, all your ideas and intentions relative to a satisfactory completion of this interesting undertaking.

12. We also recommend, that as frequent an exchange take place as conveniently may be of the observations made in the two ships; that any scientific discovery made by the one, be as quickly as possible communicated for the advantage and guidance of the other, in making their future observations, and to increase the probability of the observations of both being preserved.

13. We have caused a great variety of valuable instruments to be put on board the ships under your orders, of which you will be furnished with a list, and for the return of which you will be held responsible; among these, are instruments of the latest improvements for making a series of observations on terrestrial magnetism, which are at this time peculiarly desirable, and strongly recommended by the President and Council of the Royal Society, that the important advantage be derived from observations taken in the North Polar Sea, in co-operation with the observers who are at

present carrying out a uniform system at the magnetic observatories established by England in her distant territories, and, through her influence, in other parts of the world; and the more desirable is this co-operation in the present year, when these splendid establishments, which do so much honour to the nations who have cheerfully erected them at a great expense, are to cease. The only magnetical observations that have been obtained very partially in the Arctic Regions, are now a quarter of a century old, and it is known that the phenomena are subject to considerable secular changes. It is also stated by Colonel Sabine, that the instruments and methods of observation have been so greatly improved, that the earlier observations are not to be named in point of precision with those which would now be made; and he concludes by observing, that the passage through the Polar Sea would afford the most important service that now remains to be performed towards the completion of the magnetic survey of the globe.

14. Impressed with the importance of this subject, we have deemed it proper to request Lieut.-Colonel Sabine to allow Commander Fitzjames to profit by his valuable instructions, and we direct you, therefore, to place this important branch of science under the immediate charge of Commander Fitzjames; and as several other officers have also received similar instruction at Woolwich, you will therefore cause observations to be made daily on board each of the ships whilst at sea (and when not prevented by weather, and other circumstances) on the magnetic variation, dip and intensity, noting at the time the temperature of the air, and of the sea at the surface, and at different depths; and you will be careful that in harbour and on other favourable occasions those observations shall be attended to, by means of which the influence of the ship's iron on the result obtained at sea may be computed and allowed for.

15. In the possible event of the ships being detained during a winter in the high latitudes, the expedition has been supplied with a portable observatory, and with instruments similar to those which are employed in the fixed magnetical and meteorological observatories instituted by Her Majesty's Government in several of the British colonies.

16. It is our desire that, in the case of such detention, observations should be made with these instruments, according to the system adopted in the aforesaid observatories, and detailed directions will

be supplied for this purpose, which, with the instruction received at Woolwich, will be found, as we confidently anticipate, to afford full and sufficient guidance for such observations, which will derive from their locality peculiar interest, and a high theoretical value.

17. We have also directed instruments to be specially provided for observations on atmospherical refraction at very low altitudes, in case of the expedition being detained during a winter in the high latitudes; on this subject also particular directions will be supplied, and you will add any other meteorological observations that may occur to you of general utility; you will also take occasions to try the depth of the sea and nature of the bottom, the rise, direction and strength of the tides, and the set and velocity of currents.

18. And you are to understand that although the effecting a passage from the Atlantic to the Pacific is the main object of this expedition, yet, that the ascertaining the true geographical position of the different points of land near which you may pass, so far as can be effected without detention of the ships in their progress westward, as well as such other observations as you may have opportunities of making in natural history, geography, etc. in parts of the globe either wholly unknown or little visited, must prove most valuable and interesting to the science of our country; and we therefore desire you to give your unremitting attention, and to call that of all the officers under your command to these points, as being objects of high interest and importance.

19. For the purpose, not only of ascertaining the set of the currents in the Arctic Seas, but also of affording more frequent chances of hearing of your progress, we desire that you do frequently, after you have passed the latitude of 65° north, and once every day when you shall be in an ascertained current, throw overboard a bottle or copper cylinder closely sealed, and containing a paper stating the date and position at which it is launched, and you will give similar orders to the commander of the "Terror," to be executed in case of separation; and for this purpose, we have caused each ship to be supplied with papers, on which is printed, in several languages, a request that whoever may find it should take measures for transmitting it to this office.

20. You are to make use of every means in your power to collect and

preserve specimens of the animal, mineral and vegetable king-doms, should circumstances place such within your reach without causing your detention, and of the larger animals you are to cause accurate drawings to be made, to accompany and elucidate the descriptions of them. In this, as well as in every other part of your scientific duty, we trust that you will receive material assistance from the officers under your command, several of whom are repre-sented to us as well qualified in these respects.

21. In the event of any irreparable accident happening to either of the two ships, you are to cause the officers and crew of the disabled ship to be removed into the other, and with her singly to proceed in prosecution of the voyage, or return to England, according as circumstances shall appear to require, understanding that the officers and crew of both ships are hereby authorized and required to continue to perform the duties according to their respective ranks and stations on board either ship to which they may be so removed, in the event of an occurrence of this nature. Should, unfortunately, your own ship be the one disabled, you are in that case to take command of the "Terror," and in the event of any fatal accident happening to yourself, Captain Crozier is hereby authorized to take the command of the "Erebus," placing the officer of the expedition who may then be next in seniority to him in command of the "Terror." Also, in the event of your own ina-bility, by sickness or otherwise, at any period of this service, to con-tinue to carry these instructions into execution, you are to transfer them to the officer the next in command to you employed on the expedition, who is hereby required to execute them in the best manner he can for the attainment of the several objects herein set forth.

22. You are, while executing the service pointed out in these instruc-tions, to take every opportunity that may offer of acquainting our secretary, for our information, with your progress, and on your arrival in England you are immediately to repair to this office, in order to lay before us a full account of your proceedings in the whole course of your voyage, taking care before you leave the ship to demand from the officers, petty officers, and all other persons on board, the logs and journals they may have kept, together with any drawings or charts they may have made, which are all to be sealed up, and you will issue similar directions to Captain Crozier

and his officers. The said logs, journals or other documents to be thereafter disposed of as we may think proper to determine.

23. In the event of England becoming involved in hostilities with any other power during your absence, you are nevertheless clearly to understand that you are not on any account to commit any hostile act whatsoever, the expedition under your orders being only intended for the purpose of discovery and science, and it being the practice of all civilized nations to consider vessels so employed as excluded from the operations of war; and, confiding in this feeling, we should trust that you would receive every assistance from the ships or subjects of any foreign power which you may fall in with; but special application to that effect has been made to the respective governments.

Given under our hands, this 5th day of May 1845.

(signed) Haddington.
G. Cockburn.
W.H. Gage.

Sir John Franklin, K.C.H.,
Captain of H.M.S. "Erebus," at Woolwich.
By command of their Lordships.
(signed) W.A.B. Hamilton.

APPENDIX TWO

P.P. Vol. XLI, 1847-48. Paper 264, pp 7–9.

Copy of Instructions to Lieutenant (now Commander) Thomas E.L. Moore, commanding Her Majesty's Brig "Plover," dated 3 January 1848, —

By the Commissioners for executing the Office of Lord High Admiral, etc.

Whereas Her Majesty's Government have thought proper to adopt a plan for attempting to afford relief by way of Bhering's Strait to the Expedition in the Arctic Seas, under the command of Captain Sir John Franklin, and with this view, we have appointed you to the command of Her Majesty's brig "Plover," which vessel has been expressly fitted out for the above service, and supplied with all that is considered necessary or desirable for the wants and comforts of your crew, you are hereby required and directed, as soon as the "Plover" is, in all respects, ready, to put to sea in her, and to make the best of your way to Panama, touching only at such places on your way as may be necessary to replenish your water, and to procure the necessary refreshments for your crew, of which the Falkland Islands should be one.

By the instructions to Captain Sir John Franklin, he has been directed to communicate with the British Consul at Panama, in the event of his having succeeded in passing through Bhering's Strait, and you will there learn if any information has been received respecting the Expedition under his command.

At Panama you may expect to be joined by Her Majesty's ship "Herald," the captain of which ship has been directed to repair to that place in proper time to meet the "Plover," and the "Herald" will take on board such provisions and stores as may be required for the service in which she is about to be employed; and if no tidings of Captain Sir John Franklin's Expedition having passed through Bhering's Strait have been received, you are to proceed in the "Plover," in company with the "Herald," to Petropaulowski, for the purpose of procuring interpreters. The Russians of that place being on friendly terms, and in the habit of trading with the natives of Kotzebue Sound, would be eminently useful, by explaining to the natives the purpose for which the vessels had arrived in their neighbourhood, and introducing you to their friendship; the collisions which have taken place with these otherwise inoffensive people having invariably arisen from not understanding each other's intentions, and a mutual want of confidence.

The ships could also be supplied with fresh beef and other refreshments at this place, and application has been made to the Russian government to further the object in view, in which the interests of science and humanity are equally concerned, and orders will probably be given to the Governors of Kamschatka and Petropaulowski to afford all necessary facilities to the Expedition, and, above all, to provide it with two or three interpreters, to serve as the medium of communication with the wilder tribes of Esquimaux.

The "Herald" and "Plover" are then to proceed to Bhering's

Strait, and should arrive there about the 1st of July, and proceed along the American coast, as far as possible consistent with the certainty of preventing the ships being beset by the ice. Four whale-boats should then be despatched along the coast to look for a harbour in which to secure the "Plover" for the winter; Wainwright inlet might possibly serve for this purpose; but Captain Beechey being of a contrary opinion, you will, in the prosecution of your search after a secure harbour, merely take such steps as shall serve to satisfy yourself on this point.

The several inlets along the coast having been examined, and any one of them found suitable, two of the boats should conduct the "Plover" to her harbour, and the other two proceed along the coast in search of the voyagers, and to communicate, if possible with the party which it is intended shall descend Mackenzie River, under the command of Sir John Richardson: whale-boats, or the Russian "baidar," which you may furnish yourselves with at Petropaulowski, are better adapted for exploration along the coast, and amongst ice, than a heavy launch, on account of the facility with which their crews can haul their own boats upon the ice, or on the beach, out of danger of the pressure, and mutually assist each other.

So soon as symptoms of approaching winter should appear, the boats should return to the "Plover," which ship being fitted with fuel, and provisions and stores from the "Herald," will house in, and make all snug for the winter.

The "Herald" will then return to the southward, to give intelligence of the spot in which she left the "Plover," and then resume her surveying duties.

With the assistance of the Natives, whose friendship on this account it will be desirable to conciliate, to act as guides, construct snow-houses, and kill seals, extensive excursions are to be made early in the spring by small parties from the "Plover," in every possible and practicable direction from her winter station; but as soon as the water has formed along the coast, boat expeditions are to be again dispatched towards the Mackenzie River, again to communicate, if possible, with Sir John Richardson's party.

If no harbour fit for the "Plover" to winter in should be found to the northward of Icy Cape, search must be made more to the southward, and finally, if still unsuccessful, you must take up your winter quarters in some one of the well-protected coves of Kotzebue Sound, a place to which Sir John Franklin would be very likely to direct his steps, from its having been the appointed place of rendezvous when the "Blossom" was sent to meet him. From this position, too, it is probable that parties of Esquimaux might be induced to travel throughout the winter, when Europeans could not attempt it, and thus keep up a communication along a great extent of the coast line of the American Continent.

Your intercourse with the natives in the neighbourhood of Kotzebue Sound, should be conducted with courtesy and frankness on the one hand, but with great caution on the other, especially on your first approaches, the people on this part of the country differing in character from the ordinary Esquimaux, and being comparatively a fierce, agile and suspicious race, well armed with knives, etc., for offence, and prone to attack.

When the month of July 1849 arrives, the "Herald" will again proceed to communicate with the "Plover," and the captain of the "Herald" will be guided by his own discretion and judgement, the information he may receive, and other existing circumstances, in re-equipping the "Plover" for passing a second winter on that part of the coast, and for her repeating the above operations for the search after and for the relief of Sir John Franklin and his party or otherwise, withdrawing her in sufficient time to be clear of Bhering's Strait before the ice packs, or the winter has set in.

It will be obvious to the captain of the "Herald" that for this purpose his visit to the "Plover" in 1849 must be sufficiently early to place beyond a doubt her passing back to the westward in time to secure the passage through the Straits.

The "Plover" having been supplied with as large a quantity of preserved meats, soups and vegetables, as she can carry, in addition to the necessary provisions for her own crew during the outward voyage, you will cause these preserved meats, etc., to be reserved chiefly for the supply of the ships of Sir John Franklin's expedition, or for their crews, if compelled to abandon their ships, and travel over the ice, or along the coast of America to Bhering's Strait. The "Plover" has also been supplied with warm clothing, and such other means of comfort and defence against the severity of the climate as have been usually supplied to vessels destined to winter in high latitudes, as well as the means of warming and ventilating the ship; and various articles of utility and ornament (especially blue beads) have been put on board as presents to the natives, by which to conciliate their friendship, and obtain their assistance.

In the event of your falling in with the expedition under the command of Captain Sir John Franklin, you are to follow his orders for your further proceedings; and if, on the other hand, you should receive intelligence on which you can rely that the expedition has passed through Bhering's Strait, or returned home, you will lose no time in repairing to Panama for a confirmation of such intelligence, and, if correct, you will make the best of your way to Valparaiso to join Rear Admiral Hornby, Commander-in-Chief of Her Majesty's ships in the Pacific, and follow his orders for your further proceedings.

In an undertaking of this description much must, of course, be always left to the discretion of the commanding officer; and as the objects of the expedition have been fully explained to you, and you have already had some experience in service of this nature, we are convinced we cannot do better than leave it to your own judgement to take the best means in your power to afford the desired relief to Sir John Franklin's Expedition, always recollecting our anxiety for the health, comfort and safety of yourself, your officers and men.

You are to make the best use of every means in your power to collect and preserve specimens of the animal, mineral and vegetable kingdoms, should circumstances place such within your reach, without causing your detention.

You are, while executing the service pointed out in these Instructions, to take every opportunity that may offer of acquainting our secretary, for our information, with your proceedings, and at the termination of the above service you are to demand from the officers, petty officers and all other persons on board, the logs and journals they may have kept, together with any drawings or charts they may have kept, which are all to be sealed up, the said logs,

196

journals and other documents to be thereafter disposed of as we think proper to determine.

In the event of Great Britain becoming involved in hostilities during your absence, you are, nevertheless, clearly to understand, that you are not to commit any act of hostility whatsoever, the expedition under your orders being only intended to further the interests of science and humanity; and it being the practice of all civilized nations to consider vessels so employed as excluded from the operations of war, and, confiding in this general feeling, we should trust that you will receive every assistance from the ships and subjects of any foreign power you may fall in with.

Some valuable memoranda on subjects relating to the navigation and service in which you are to be engaged have been presented to us by Captain Beechey, and a copy of these is added for your further guidance and instruction.

Given, etc., 3rd January 1848.

(signed) Auckland
John Hay

To Lieut. Thos. E.L. Moore,
Commanding H.M. Brig "Plover,"
    at Plymouth.

By command, etc. (signed) H.G. Ward.

APPENDIX THREE

P.P. Vol. XLI, 1847-48, Paper 386. *A "COPY of the Orders from the Lords Commissioners of the Admiralty, under which Captain Sir James Clark Ross, R.N., has proceeded on an Expedition in search of Captain Sir John Franklin, R.N."*

By the Commissioners for executing the Office of Lord High Admiral of the United Kingdom of Great Britain and Ireland, etc.

Whereas the period for which Her Majesty's ships "Erebus" and "Terror" were victualled will terminate at the end of this summer;

and whereas no tidings whatever of the proceedings of either of those ships have reached us since their first entry into Lancaster Sound, in the year 1845, and there being, therefore, reason to apprehend that they may have been blocked up by immoveable ice, and that they may soon be exposed to suffer great privation; we have deemed it proper to defer no longer the endeavour to afford them adequate relief. Having, therefore, caused to be prepared and duly equipped, with extra stores and provisions, two suitable vessels, and having had them properly fortified, so as to resist the pressure of the ice, and having the fullest confidence in the skill and experience that you have acquired in those inclement seas, we have thought proper to place them under your command; and you are hereby required and directed, so soon as they are in all respects ready for sea, to proceed in the "Enterprize," under your immediate command, and taking the "Investigator" (Captain Bird) under your orders, without delay to Lancaster Sound. In your progress through that inlet to the westward, you will carefully search both its shores, as well as those of Barrow Straits, for any notices that may have been deposited there, and for any casual indications of their having been visited by either of Sir John Franklin's ships.

Should your early arrival there, or the fortunately protracted openness of the season, admit of your at once extending a similar examination to the shores of the Wellington Channel, it will leave you at greater liberty to devote yourself more fully afterwards to your researches to the westward. The several intervals of coast that appear in our charts to lie between Capes Clarence and Walker, must next be carefully explored; and as each of your vessels have been furnished with a launch fitted with a small engine and screw, capable of propelling it between four and five knots, we trust by their means, or by the ships' boats, all those preliminary researches may be completed during the present season, and consequently before it may be necessary to secure the ships in safety previous to the approaching winter. As that winter may possibly prove to be so severe as to seal up the western end of that extensive inlet, and as it would be unwise to allow both vessels to be beset there, we consider that it would be prudent to look out for a fit and safe port near Cape Rennell, and in that neighbourhood to secure the "Investigator" for the ensuing winter. From that position a considerable extent of coast may be explored on foot, and in the following spring detached parties may be sent across the ice by Captain

Bird, in order to look thoroughly into the creeks along the western coast of Bosthia, Boothia and even as far as Cape Nicolai; while another party may proceed to the southward, and ascertain whether the blank space shown there in our charts consists of an open sea through which Sir John Franklin may have passed, or, on the contrary, of a continuous chain of Islands, among which he may be still blocked up. As soon as the returning summer shall have opened a passage between the land and the main body of the ice, this eastern vessel is to detach her steam-launch to Lancaster Sound, in order to meet the whale ships which usually visit the western side of Baffin Bay about that time, and by which we purpose to send out further instructions and communications to you, as well as to receive in return an account of your proceedings.

The "Enterprize" in the meantime will press forward to the westward, and endeavour to reach Winter Harbour in Melville Island, or perhaps, if circumstances should in your judgement render it advisable, to push onward to Banks' Land; but in either case a distinct statement of the measures you are going to adopt, as well as of your future intentions, should be deposited in some spot previously communicated to Captain Bird. From this western station you will be able to spread some active parties, and to make some short and useful excursions before the season altogether closes, and still more effective ones in the ensuing spring. One party should then pursue the coast in whatever direction it may seem likely to have been followed by Sir John Franklin, and thus determine the general shape of the western face of Banks' Land. It is then to proceed direct to Cape Bathurst or to Cape Parry on the main land, at each of which places we have directed Sir J. Richardson to leave provisions for its use; that party will then advance to Fort Good Hope, where they will find directions for continuing their progress up the M'Kenzie River, so as to return to England by the usual route of traders.

Another party will explore the eastern coast of Banks' Land, and from thence make at once for Cape Krusenstern, where, or at Cape Hearne, a cache of Pemmican will be placed for Sir John Richardson.

They should communicate immediately with him, according to the agreement which he and you have made, and, placing themselves under his orders, they will assist him in examining the shores of Victoria and Wollaston's Islands, and finally return with him to England, by whatever route he may deem advisable. Unable to foresee the variety of circumstances in which you may be placed, or the difficulties with which you may have to contend, and fully relying on the skillfulness of your measures, as well as by the zeal with which you and those under your command will be animated, we direct you to consider the foregoing orders as the general outline only of our desires, and not as intended too rigidly to control your proceedings, especially whenever, after due deliberation, you have become satisfied that the end we have in view may be more certainly accomplished by the substitution of some other course of operations; and if Providence should not be pleased to crown your efforts with success, we leave it to your own judgement when and from whence to return to England, as soon as you are convinced that every means within your reach have been exhausted.

In case of any irreparable accident happening to the "Enterprize," you are hereby authorized to take the command of the "Investigator," and to make such arrangements for the officers and crew as may be most consonant to the rules of the service, and most conductive to the objects of the expedition.

If you should happily succeed in meeting with the "Erebus" afloat and Sir John Franklin's pendant be flying, you will of course place yourself under his orders; but if you should find that ship blocked up with ice, or otherwise incapable of proceeding, you are hereby authorized and directed to retain the command of the expedition, and adopt all such measures as may be requisite for the safe removal of her crew, or that of the "Terror."

In the event of Great Britain being involved in hostilities with any foreign power during your absence, you are to abstain from the smallest act of aggression towards any vessel belonging to such nation, it being the practice of all civilized countries to consider vessels engaged on service of this kind as exempt from the rules and operations of war. Both vessels under your orders have been furnished with abundance of stores, and with more than a sufficiency of every thing that can in anywise contribute to the welfare of their crews; and we especially direct you to consider their safety, health and comfort as predominant in every operation that you undertake. Each of them has likewise been supplied with numerous instruments for the purpose of making geographic, hydrographic, magnetic and atmospheric observations in those northern and rarely visited regions of the globe; and we annex hereto a copy of the instructions given to Sir J. Franklin, in order that you may pursue a similar course; and though we estimate any such observations as of inferior importance to the one leading object of the expedition, you will, nevertheless, omit no opportunity of rendering it as contributive to scientific acquisition as to the performance of the great duties of national humanity. In carrying out the above orders, you will avail yourself of every practical occasion of acquainting our Secretary with every step of your progress, as well with your future intentions; and on your reaching England you will call on every person in both vessels to deliver up to you all their logs, journals, charts and drawings, but which, they may be informed, shall be returned to them in due time.

Given under our hands this 9th day of May 1848.

> (signed) Auckland.
> J.W.D. Dundas.

Sir Jas. C. Ross,
Captain of H.M. Ship "Enterprize,"
Greenhithe.

> By command of their Lordships.
> (signed) H.G. Ward.

APPENDIX FOUR

P.P., Vol. XLI, 1847–48, Paper 264, pp 19–21.

Instructions to Sir John Richardson, M.D., 16th. March 1848. By the Commissioners for executing the office of Lord High Admiral, etc.

Whereas we think fit that you should be employed on an overland expedition in search of Her Majesty's ships "Erebus" and "Terror," under the command of Captain Sir John Franklin, which ships are engaged in a voyage of discovery in the Arctic seas, you are hereby required and directed to take under your orders Mr. Rae, who has been selected to accompany you, and to leave England on the 25th instant by the mail steamer for Halifax, Nova

Scotia and New York, and on your arrival at the latter place, you are to proceed immediately to Montreal, for the purpose of conferring with Sir George Simpson, Governor of the Hudson's Bay Company's Settlements, and making arrangements with him for your future supplies and communications.

You should next travel to Penetanguishene, on Lake Huron, and from thence, by a steamer, which sails on the 1st and 15th of every month of open water, to Sault St. Marie, at the Fort [foot] of Lake Superior, and there embark in a canoe, which, with its crew, will have been provided for you by that time by Sir George Simpson.

Following the usual canoe route by Fort William, Rainy Lake, the Lake of the Woods, Lake Winipeg (sic) and the Saskatchewan River, it is hoped that you will overtake the boats, now under charge of Mr. Bell, in July 1848, somewhere near Isle à la Crosse, or perhaps the Metley (sic) Portage.
You will then send the canoe with its crew back to Canada, and having stowed the four boats for their sea voyage, you will go on as rapidly as you can to the mouth of the Mackenzie, leaving Mr. Bell to follow with the heavier laden barge, to turn off at Great Bear Lake, and erect your winter residence at Fort Confidence, establish fisheries, and send out hunters.

Making a moderate allowance for unavoidable detention by ice, thick fogs and storms, the examination of the coast between the Mackenzie and the Coppermine Rivers will probably occupy 30 days, but you cannot calculate to be able to keep the sea latter (sic) than the 15th of September, for from the beginning of that month, the young ice covers the sea almost every night, and very greatly impedes the boats, until the day is well advanced.

If you reach the sea in the first week of August, it is hoped you will be able to make the complete voyage to the Coppermine River, and also to coast a considerable part of the western and southern shores of Wollaston Land, and to ascend the Coppermine to some convenient point, where Mr. Bell and a party can be left with the provisions ready for the next year's voyage; and you will instruct him to send two hunters to the banks of the river to provide food for the party on the route to Fort Confidence, and thus spare you any further consumption of pemmican, reserved for the following summer.

As it may happen, however, from your late arrival on the coast, or subsequent unexpected detentions, that you cannot with safety attempt to reach the Coppermine, you have our full permission in such a case to return to Fort Good Hope, on the Mackenzie, there to deposit two of the boats, with all the sea stores, and to proceed with the other two boats, and the whole of the crews, to winter quarters on Great Bear Lake.

And you have also our permission to deviate from the line of route along the coast, should you receive accounts from the Esquimaux, which may appear credible, of the crews of the "Erebus" and "Terror," or some part of them, being in some other direction.

For the purpose of more widely extending your search, you are at liberty to leave Mr. Rae and a party of volunteers to winter on the coast, if by the establishment of a sufficient fishery, or by killing a number of deer or musk oxen, you may be able to lay up provisions enough for them until you can rejoin them next summer.

As you have been informed by Captain Sir James Ross, of Her Majesty's Ship "Enterprize," who is about to be employed on a similar search in another direction, of the probable directions in which the parties he will send out towards the continent will travel, you are to leave a deposit of pemmican for their use at the following points; namely, Point Separation, Cape Bathurst, Cape Parry, and Cape Krusenstern; and as Sir James Ross is desirous that some pemmican should be stored at Fort Good Hope, for the use of a party which he purposes sending thither in the spring of 1849, and which party, not being able to ascend the river, you are to make the necessary arrangements with Sir George Simpson for that purpose, as his directions to that effect to the Company's servants must be sent early enough to meet the Company's brigade of Mackenzie River boats at Portage la Roche (sic), in July 1848.

Should it appear necessary to continue the search a second summer (1849), and should the boats have been housed on the Coppermine, you are to descend that river on the breaking up of the ice in June 1849, and to examine the passages between Wollaston and Banks and Victoria Lands, so as to cross the routes of some of Sir James C. Ross's detached parties, and to return to Great Bear Lake in September 1849, and withdraw the whole party from thence to winter on Great Slave Lake, which would be as far south as you will have a prospect of travelling before the close of the river navigation.

Should you have found it necessary to return to the Mackenzie (September 1848), instead of pushing on to the Coppermine, the search in the summer of 1849 would, of course, have to be commenced from the former river again; but should circumstances render it practicable and desirable to send some of the party down the Coppermine with one or two boats, you are at liberty to do so.

A passage for yourself and Mr. Rae will be provided in the "America," British and North American mail-steamer, which sails from Liverpool on the 25th of March, and you will receive a letter of credit on Her Majesty's Consul at New York for the amount of the expense of your journey from New York to Sault St. Marie, and the carriage of the instruments, etc.

And in the event of intelligence of the "Erebus" and "Terror" reaching England after your departure, a communication will be made to the Hudson's Bay Company to ascertain the most expeditious route to forward your recall.

We consider it scarcely necessary to furnish you with any instructions contingent on a successful search after the above-mentioned expedition, or any parties belonging to it.

The circumstances of the case, and your own local knowledge and experience, will best point out the means to be adopted for the speedy transmission to this country to the above effect, as well as of aiding and directing in the return of any such parties to England.

We are only anxious that the search so laudably undertaken by you and your colleagues should not be unnecessarily or hazardously prolonged; and whilst we are confident that no pains or labour will be spared in the execution of this service, we fear lest the zeal and anxiety of the party so employed may carry them farther than would be otherwise prudent.

It is on this account you are to understand that your search is not to be prolonged after the winter of 1849, and which will be passed on the Great Slave Lake; but that at the earliest practicable moment after the breaking up of the weather in the spring of 1850, you will take such steps for the return of the party under your orders to England as circumstances may render expedient.

It must be supposed that the instructions now afforded you can scarcely meet every contingency that may arise out of a service of the above description; but reposing, as we do, the utmost confidence in your discretion and judgement, you are not only at liberty to deviate from any point of them that may seem at variance with the objects of the expedition, but you are further empowered to take such other steps as shall be desirable at the time, and which are not provided for in these orders.

Given under our hands, 16th March 1848.

> (signed) Auckland.
> J.W.D. Dundas.

To Sir John Richardson, M.D., etc.
By command, etc.
> (signed) W.A.B. Hamilton.

APPENDIX FIVE

P.P. Vol. XLI, 1847-48, Paper 264, pp 16 – 18.

Admiralty orders to Captain Henry Kellett, R.N., of H.M.S. Herald, dated 13 December 1847.

INSTRUCTIONS to Captain Kellett, Her Majesty's Ship "Herald."

13 December 1847.

Sir,

My Lords Commissioners of the Admiralty being about to adopt a plan of affording relief to the Expedition in the Arctic Seas, under the command of Captain Sir John Franklin, by way of Bhering's Strait, and Her Majesty's ship "Plover" being now fitted out for this service, under the command of Lieutenant T.E.L. Moore, I am commanded by their Lordships to acquaint you, that the "Plover" will sail from England for Cape Horn and Panama about the first of January 1848, and may be expected to arrive at Panama about May next. My Lords desire, that towards the end of April or beginning of May next you will repair in the "Herald" to Panama to meet the "Plover," and if no tidings of Captain Sir John Franklin having passed through Bhering's Strait have been received, you are to take on board as much provision and store as may be required for the service, and you are to proceed with the "Herald," in company with the "Plover," to Petropaulowski, for the purpose of procuring interpreters: the Russians of that place being on friendly terms, and in the habit of trading with the nations of Kotzebue Sound, would be eminently useful, by explaining to the natives the purpose for which the vessels had arrived in their neighbourhood, and introducing them to their friendship; the collisions that have taken place with these otherwise inoffensive people having invariably arisen from not understanding each other's intentions, and mutual want of confidence. The ships could also be supplied with fresh beef and other refreshments at this place; and application has been made to the Russian Government to further this object in view, in which the interests of science and humanity are equally concerned; and orders will probably be sent to the Governors of Kamschatka and Petropaulowski to afford all necessary facilities to the expedition, and, above all, to provide it with two or three interpreters to serve as the medium of communication with the wilder tribes of Esquimaux. The "Herald" and the "Plover" are then to proceed to Bhering's Strait, and should arrive there about the 1st of July, and proceed along the American coast as far as possible consistent with the certainty of preventing the ships being beset by the ice. Four whale-boats should then be despatched along the coast to look for a harbour, in which to secure the "Plover" for the winter; Wainwright Inlet appears well adapted for the purpose, if there is a sufficient depth of water. The several inlets along the coast having been examined, and any one of them found suitable, two of the boats should return to conduct the "Plover" to her harbour, and the other two proceed along the coast in search of voyagers, and to communicate, if possible, with the party which it is intended should descend the Mackenzie River under the command of Sir John Richardson. Whale-boats, or the Russian baidar, which you may furnish yourselves with at Petropaulowski, are better adapted for exploration along the coast and amongst ice than a heavy launch, on account of the facility with which their crews can haul their boats up on the ice or the beach out of danger of the pressure, and mutually assist each other. As soon as symptoms of approaching winter should appear, the boats should return to the "Plover," which ship being fitted with fuel and provisions and stores from the "Herald," will house in and make all snug for the winter: the "Herald" is then to return to the southward, to give intelligence of the spot in which she left the "Plover," and then resume her surveying duties. With the assistance of the natives, whose friendship on this account especially it will be desirable to conciliate, to act as guides, construct snow-houses, and kill seals, extensive excursions will be made early in the spring by small parties from the "Plover," in every desirable direction from the winter station; but as soon as the water has formed along the coast, boat expeditions will be again despatched towards the Mackenzie River, again to communicate, if possible, with Sir John Richardson's party. When the month of July again arrives, you are to proceed in the "Herald" to communicate with the "Plover," and you will be guided by your own judgement and discretion, the information you may receive, and other existing circumstances, in re-equipping the "Plover," for passing another winter in that part of the coast, and for her repeating the above operations for the search after and relief of Sir John Franklin, or otherwise withdrawing her in sufficient time to be clear of Bhering's Strait before the ice packs, or the winter has set in. It will be obvious to you, that for this purpose your visit to the "Plover" must be sufficiently early to place beyond a doubt her passing back to the westward in time to secure her passage through the Strait. You are to communicate to me, for their Lordships' information, by every possible opportunity, all your proceedings while employed on the above service.

(signed) H.G. Ward.

Captain Henry Kellett, C.B.,
Her Majesty's Ship "Herald," Panama.

7 January 1848.

Sir,
With reference to that part of my letter to you of the 13th December last, in which you are directed to proceed in the "Herald" in company with the "Plover" to Petropaulowski, and from thence to Bhering's Straits, I am commanded by my Lords Commissioners

of the Admiralty to acquaint you, that Lieutenant Moore is to be permitted to proceed with the "Plover" from Panama to an appointed rendezvous at the entrance of Bhering's Strait direct, while the "Herald" proceeds to Petropaulowski for the interpreters, and then rejoin the "Plover" at such place as shall have been fixed upon by yourself and Lieutenant Moore conjointly.

(signed) I have, etc.,
H.G. Ward.

Captain Kellett, C.B.,
Her Majesty's Ship "Herald."

FURTHER INSTRUCTIONS to Captain Kellett, Her Majesty's Ship "Herald."

Admiralty, 10 March 1848.

Sir,

I am commanded by my Lords Commissioners of the Admiralty to send you herewith a copy of a letter from Lord Bloomfield, Her Majesty's ambassador at St. Petersburgh, dated 29th January last, addressed to Viscount Palmerston, transmitting an extract of a letter from Admiral Lutke, together with a letter addressed to the Governor of Sitka, and certain charts, and a book of sailing instructions for the use of Her Majesty's ship "Plover;" and I am to desire you, with reference to former orders, to be guided by the information contained in the paper marked (B) as to your proceeding to Norton Sound, and in the delivery of the letter to the Governor of Sitka, and you are to arrange for Commander Moore, of the "Plover," being made fully aware of your intentions touching such means for his being provided with the charts and sailing instructions as may seem to you to be most practicable and expedient.

(signed) I am, etc.,
H.G. Ward.

Captain Kellett, C.B.,
Her Majesty's Ship "Herald," Panama.

208

Foreign Office,
18 February 1848.

Sir,

With reference to your letter of the 7th December last, I am directed by Viscount Palmerston to transmit to you, for the information of the Lords Commissioners of the Admiralty, a copy of a despatch from Lord Bloomfield, together with certain letters and charts which have been presented for the use of Her Majesty's ship "Plover."

(signed) I am, etc.,
H.M. Addington.

Captain Hamilton, R.N.

St. Petersburgh, 29 January 1848.

My Lord,

With reference to my despatch, No.248, of the 22nd ultimo, acquainting your Lordship that the Russian Government would transmit instructions to the authorities at Kamschatka and Petropaulowski, to afford every assistance in their power to the expedition which has left England in search of Sir John Franklin, I have the honour to state, that I have had some conversation on this subject with Admiral Lutke, the Vice-President of the Russian Geographical Society, and that his Excellency is of opinion that little or no assistance could be afforded to the expedition at the abovementioned places, and that the interpreters or guides which it may require ought to be taken from a small factory of the Russian-American Company in Norton Sound.

The Admiral subsequently addressed a letter to me, of which I enclose an extract, recapitulating his views on this subject; and, in conformity with his suggestions, I have communicated with Ct. Nesselrode, and have obtained, through his Excellency's good offices, a letter, which I have the honour to transmit herewith, from the directors of the Russian American Company, instructing the Governor of Sitka in Norfolk Sound to do everything in his power to forward the objects of the expedition, and to furnish the Commander of Her Majesty's ship "Plover" with orders to obtain any interpreters he may require at the establishment of the Company in Norton Sound.

Admiral Lutke, who is acquainted with the localities from personal observation, has also had the goodness to forward to me, for transmission to the Commander of the "Plover," the two accompanying packets, No.1. containing charts, and No.2. a book of sailing instructions, in the hope that they may prove useful to that officer in the performance of the interesting duty with which he has been charged.

In concluding this despatch, I feel called upon not merely to express my sense of the readiness with which the requests of Her Majesty's Government with respect to this subject have been complied with by the Imperial authorities, as I have already had the honour to acquaint your Lordship, but also to record the anxious desire which they have manifested to contribute, by every means at their disposal, to the successful issue of the enterprise on which the "Plover" has sailed to Bhering's Straits.

(signed) I am, etc.,
Bloomfield.

APPENDIX SIX

P.R.O. Adm.7/189. *Commander T.E.L. Moore's orders to Lieutenant W.J.S. Pullen, commanding the Boat Expedition, dated 25 July 1849.*

By Thomas E.L. Moore, Esquire,
Commander of Her Majesty's Brig Plover.

You are hereby required and directed to proceed with the decked boats of the *Herald* and *Plover* accompanied by two whalers, in the route which I shall point out to you in these instructions, taking under your orders Mr. Wm. H. Hooper, acting Mate, Mr. H. Martin, second master, and John Abernethy, acting second master Ice.

The boats will be victualled for 70 days, besides which each will take 5 cases of Pemmican to be disposed of as I shall hereafter direct.

After you have satisfied yourself that your boats are in every respect provided with the necessary stores, provisions, etc., you will make the best of your way towards the Mackenzie River (first touching at Refuge Inlet to insure a retreat for the decked boats should you be unable to proceed in them) prosecuting your voyage in the smaller boats, and sending the decked ones back to Refuge Inlet, in charge of Mr. Hooper, with instructions to him to remain there as long as he possibly can for your return, but to bury a part of his provisions and proceed to sea on the appearance of ice in the Inlet keeping as close to it as he possibly can.

You are to keep the land as close on board as you can consistently do with safety, so that you may be enabled to notice any marks which may have been left by the party of which you are in search.

On your arrival at the head of the delta of the Mackenzie, you will visit Point Separation in Latitude 67° 38′ N., Longitude 133° 53′ W., and Whale Island at the north of the Mackenzie, at which places you will find landmarks of wood or stone, painted either white or red or with black stripes, and also faces of rock similarly marked, and bottles buried in the circumference of a circle drawn with a ten feet radius from the point of a broad arrow painted on the signal posts.

On obtaining any of these notes you will be guided by their contents as to the propriety of bringing them to the ship for my inspection or not, taking care to re-bury them (should you find it necessary) in such a manner that the natives may not be led to suspect that anything be concealed near the spot.

When you visit Point Separation you will bury a bottle enclosing a note, therein stating the date of your arrival and the terms of your instructions, marking the plan as distinctly as you can.

After leaving every information in your power at Point Separation, you will make the best of your way back to the *Plover*, but should you find in your journey toward the Mackenzie, that you will be unable to gain it in sufficient time to reach the ship by the 15th September, you will use your own discretion as to the best time to return, leaving marks on the most conspicuous parts of the coast, with buried information of the *Plover's* position and the proceedings of the boats.

After your arrival at the Mackenzie should you be by any unfortunate occurrence prevented from returning, you are to make for a

Post of the Hudson's Bay Company on Peel River, which falls into the Mackenzie at the head of the delta, but as no reliance can be placed on recovering supplies of Provisions there, you will pay the strictest attention to the issuing and safe keeping of the boats provisions, so that there be no loss or injury sustained.

Should you find it absolutely necessary to seek a post, it would be better if possible for you to proceed to Fort Good Hope, situated on the west or north bank of the Mackenzie, one day or one day and a half tracking above Point Separation.

The cans of pemmican with which the boats will be supplied are on no account to be opened, but for any parties of Sir John Franklin's expedition, except your own provisions fail you and you have no chance of a fresh supply.

You will occasionally land along the coast to search for any marks that may have been created, and should you meet natives, you are to glean every information in your power relative to Sir John Franklin (as you have the Interpreter with you, I trust you will have little difficulty in conversing with them) taking every precaution that you give them no offence, never making any unnecessary display of arms, or landing when any number are assembled.

With reference to your movements in case you should be prevented returning as before mentioned, after arriving at the Mackenzie, you are most distinctly to understand that although Peel River and Fort Good Hope are to be sought for by you in case of necessity, you are to use every possible endeavour to surmount any difficulties which may be thrown in your way, by encouraging them under your orders, and taking timely advantage of every favourable circumstance which may occur to return to the ship. Should however your efforts prove unavailing you will make the best of your way to York Factory, reporting yourself and party to their Lordships with as little delay as possible.

Whenever you have an opportunity (without losing a minute's time) of collecting specimens of natural history you are to do so.

You will keep a journal of your proceedings, wherein you will note any circumstance worthy of remark, which is to be directed to me on your return, with a written detail of your journey.

You will be provided with a quantity of cutlery, tobacco, beads, etc., which you will distribute among such natives as you may meet, doing everything in your power to obtain their friendship.

Should any of the notes you may obtain state that provisions can be procured at Peel River or Fort Good Hope you are to winter there, if you think it at all possible that you may meet with difficulties on your return, which would cause you to winter on the coast.

With respect to the time of your return, and the manner of proceeding, it must be left of course, entirely on your own judgement and discretion, bearing in mind that you have no prospect of obtaining supplies at either of the Posts mentioned in these orders.

I would recommend that on your arriving off Point Barrow, that you leave one or both your decked boats at that place, as I think you would accomplish the journey in a much shorter time, in the smaller boats, giving orders to Mr. Hooper to return to Refuge Inlet, or any place most convenient, so as to meet you on your return.

On your passage up, you should make arrangements as to the spot where the provisions should be buried in case of necessity.

Having the acting ice master with you, you will have the advantage of nearly 20 years experience amongst ice, which I hope will be sufficient to give you timely warning as to the approach of danger.

In conclusion I have to point out to you Icy Cape, Point Hope, and Cape Lisburne as places of rendezvous where you will meet me, or find buried information of my position, but you may be quite sure of finding me at Chamisso Island.

Having been fortunate enough to reach the Lat. of 70° 46′ N., and Wainwright Inlet proving unavailable as a winter quarters for the *Plover*, I am unavoidably prevented leaving the ship, I must therefore express a hope that every exertion will be exercised by you and your party in carrying out these orders, and the wishes of the Lords Commissioners of the Admiralty, and I shall now see you leave with full confidence in your intentions to put forth all your energy for the relief of our missing countrymen, and may you by God's help be the fortunate means of rendering them assistance, being careful of yourself and party, as you must be well aware of the anxiety which will be felt by myself and all on board on your account.

Given under my hand on board
  H.M.S. *Plover* off Wainwrights
  Inlet the 25th July 1849.

(signed) T.E.L. Moore,
Commander.

Lieutenant Pullen,
H.M.S. *Plover*.

APPENDIX SEVEN

P.R.O., Adm.7/189. *Captain Henry Kellett's instructions to Lieutenant W.J.S. Pullen, commanding the Boat Expedition, dated 25 July 1849.*

H.M.S. Herald,
Off Wainwright Inlet,
25th July 1849.

Sir,
Commander Moore having placed before me your orders for the conduct of the interesting expedition of which he has given you the command; I consider them to embrace all contingencies and therefore left but little to add. I shall swiftly send you a few extracts from the printed papers relative to the different Expeditions in the Arctic Seas, as well as one or two notes from the narrative of Dease and Simpson's voyage between the Mackenzie River and Point Barrow. [1837-39.]

A few points in your orders will I am of the opinion, require your immediate decision on your arrival with all boats at Point Barrow.

The first and most material point, is, on arriving at Point Barrow, to decide whether you will push for the Mackenzie in the light boats and send back the launches, having previously filled up with provisions from them. I hardly think it possible to go half way to the Mackenzie, and get back to join the *Plover* this season; but consider it very practicable in light boats to go direct there. Simpson did it, you perceive in 13 days, leaving Point Barrow on the 4th of August.

You will see by the accompanying extract the probability of there being provisions deposited at Fort Good Hope.

Should you decide to return, you should be south of Icy Cape by the first week in September, so says Captain Beechy, whose authority is not to be doubted.

Should you leave the heavy boats at Refuge Inlet as a rendezvous, with an intention of returning to them – you must bear in mind, that, it is more than likely in the middle of August – with the first westerly wind, they will be obliged to leave it, to escape being beset in the ice, and as Wainwright Inlet to all appearances does not afford refuge, on account of its entrance being barred, they would be obliged to make for Point Hope, where you should instruct them to rendezvous; and where, up to the 10th September they may expect to meet this ship, or find instructions deposited 10 feet magnetic north from a pole, or marked directions on some conspicuous rock or cliff.

Should you get to the Mackenzie and not return this year (which I think you should be most cautious in attempting) and determine to return next year, it will be necessary for you to be south of Point Barrow early in August 1850, to ensure meeting this ship or the *Plover*.

Trusting that through the blessings of Providence, you may be successful in the object of your expedition, and that your gallant little band may enjoy good health.

> I remain,
> Your obedient servant,
> (Sgd.) Henry Kellett, Captain.

APPENDIX EIGHT

P.R.O., Adm.7/189. *Dr. Rae to Sir John Richardson, from Fort Simpson,
5 October 1849.*

Fort Simpson,
5 October 1849.

My dear Sir John,
I little thought that another opportunity of addressing you would
occur so soon but such however is the case.

Two days ago a boat was observed tracking up the river, having a
blue flag flying, and on landing here, Lieut. Pullen of H.M. Brig
Plover stepped on shore.

It appears he left the *Plover* off Wainwright Inlet, with two large
boats and two smaller ones, having 25 men and officers under his
command. They were accompanied as far as Point Barrow by a
yacht belonging to an Englishman named Sheddon, who deserves
great credit for his perseverance in pushing on farther than the
Plover dare venture. He was also extremely kind to the searching
party and supplied them with everything that he thought might
prove useful. When some days voyage east of Pt. Barrow, there
being no ice in the way, Pullen sent back the two large boats and
came on with the two small ones, having an officer and 12 men
with him. He arrived at Peel House on the 5th Sept. where he left
Hooper (the mate) and 5 of his men who were so fatigued that
they could go no farther, fortunately some provisions were left with
them which I hope will enable Mr. Peers to support the party
until the ice is sufficiently firm to allow them to come this far,
although I do not know what we are to do with them as our stores
are almost perfectly empty of everything eatable and the fishing at
the Big Island appears less productive than usual if I may judge by
the lateness of the boats in arriving with their piscatory cargoes
from that place.

The seamen are almost completely naked; they left the ship, without any other clothes but those they had on their backs and none
of the party had a *blanket* or a *substitute* for one. Providentially they
had fine weather, and consequently did not suffer much inconvenience.

I shall do all in my power to supply the wants of the party although our means are far from being so abundant as I would wish. It is only now that the effects of the recent searching expedition visit are beginning to be felt, empty stores as I have already mentioned and not much prospect of having them soon refilled with such an additional number of mouths to feed. By some fatality also the Indians I am led to believe, have an idea that no meat is required at this place, which accounts for the very small quantity that is brought in. All I can do is to hope for the best, and use my utmost endeavours to keep all parties on full allowance throughout the winter.

Five of the men just arrived are to be shipped off for Big Island by the first opportunity; the remaining two (marines) are to stay here.

Mr. Pullen is a most agreeable man and will be a great addition to our *small* society here but I fear our mess will not be quite so well supplied as it was last winter at Fort Confidence. We shall have two *luxuries* that we had not there i.e., milk and potatoes.

I omitted to mention that the *Plover* wintered on the Asiatic Coast and the Ships' Company were well supplied with venison by the Esquimaux who have large herds of tame reindeer.

> I am your etc.,
> (Signed) John Rae.

APPENDIX NINE

P.P., Vol.XLI, 1847-48. Paper 264, pp. 64-65.

A list of the seamen who volunteered for, and took part in Sir John Richardson's overland expedition of 1848-49.

Daniel Clarke, Able Seaman, H.M.S. *St. Vincent.*
Thomas Selley, Able Seaman, H.M.S. *St. Vincent.*
William Done, Able Seaman, H.M.S. *Excellent.*
George Stares, Able Seaman, H.M.S. *Excellent.*
Thomas Cousins, Able Seaman, H.M.S. *Victory.*

P.P., Vol.XLI, 1847-48. Paper 264, p 65.

RETURN of Men of the ROYAL SAPPERS and MINERS who have been medically examined and selected by Sir John Richardson from Volunteers to accompany the Expedition for tracing the Progress of Captain Sir John Franklin to the West of Cape Walker. Woolwich, 17 May 1847.

Rank.	Name.	Trade.	Age. Yr.	M	Service. Yr.	M.	Character.
2d. Corporal.	James M'Haren.	carpenter.	28	1	6	11	very good
"	David Brodie.	carpenter.	21	3	1	-	good.
"	Robert Graham.	carpenter	25	5	7	5	good.
"	Henry J. Ralph.	carpenter.	26	7	6	9	very bad
"	Robert Mackie.	carpenter.	26	4	6	6	very good.
"	Donald Fraser.	carpenter.	25	1	1	4	good.
"	Edward Dodd.	Wood and iron-turner.	20	6	1	4	good.
"	Hugh Geddes.	painter.	19	5	1	5	good.
Privates	Richard Webber.	millwright.	23	4	1	4	good.
"	James Mitchell.	smith.	25	4	7	-	very good.
"	Jacob Hobbs.	smith.	23	9	1	2	good.
"	Thomas Bugbee.	smith.	25	5	1	5	good.
"	John Salter.	smith.	29	10	6	10	good.
"	James Waddell.	miner.	20	9	1	9	good.
"	Robert Dall.	miner.	23	9	1	5	good

H. Sandham, Brigade Major.

Extract from p. 69, Paper 264, P.P., Vol. XLI, 1847-48.

Haslar Hospital, 2 June 1847.

My dear Sir,

I was aware of the bad character of Henry Ralph, the Sapper and Miner; but having ascertained that his crime was repeated drunkeness, and that he was otherwise an obedient, hard-working man, I yielded to his request to be allowed an opportunity of reform, by employing him where no drink was to be had. The only hazard is his committing some excess before the ship leaves England, and he is physically well qualified for severe labour....

I am, etc.,
(signed) John Richardson.

Captain W.A.B. Hamilton, R.N.

P.R.O., Adm. 38/2041. *Muster List of H.M.S. Crocodile, October 1851.*
*A list of the officers, seamen and marines that formed the crews of the two 27
foot gig whale boats.*

Lieutenant W.J.S. Pullen, R.N., in command of the Boat Expedi-
tion.
Mr. W.H. Hooper, acting Mate, R.N.
*Mr. John Abernethy, acting Second Master, Ice.
John Hammett, Boatswain Mate, Sailmaker.
William Salmon, Able Seaman, Captain Main Top.
*John Senior, Able Seaman, Captain Fore Top.
James Warby, Able Seaman, Captain Fore Top.
Thomas Mellish, Able Seaman.
William Seymour, Able Seaman.
John Robinson, Able Seaman.
James Tullock, Able Seaman.
William McCarthy, Able Seaman.
John Herd, Private, Royal Marines.
Robert Tullock, Private, Royal Marines.

*Mr. Abernethy and John Senior were sent back to England, by way of York Fac-
tory and the Hudson's Bay Company's ship, medically unfit, in the summer of
1850.
N.B. All the officers, seamen, marines, sappers and miners, mentioned above, were
awarded the Arctic Medal, 1818-55. See "The White Ribbon," pp. 99–100 for the
Medal Roll.

APPENDIX TEN

P.R.O., Adm.2/1608. *Admiralty orders of 25 January 1850, to Commander Pullen to continue the search if he thought it adviseable.*

Admiralty, 25 January 1850.
Sir,
I am commanded by my Lords Commissioners of the Admiralty to
acquaint you, that Captain Sir James Ross has returned to England with the "Enterprize" and "Investigator," without having
discovered any traces of Sir John Franklin and the missing ships.

2. An expedition has been despatched to Bhering's Straits, under the

command of Captain Collinson, a copy of whose orders is herewith enclosed.

3.   With reference to despatches received from Captain Kellett, of the "Herald," dated to 22d November last, showing the probability of your being at some of the posts on the Mackenzie River, or on the Slave or Great Bear Lake, and the Governor and Committee of the Hudson's Bay Company having offered their services to forward any instructions to you, and viewing the possible opportunity which your position may afford of a search being made from Cape Bathurst towards Bank's Land, my Lords are pleased to convey to you their sanction for your prosecuting such search, if, after a mature consideration of all the circumstances of the case, you may consider it likely to be attended with beneficial results.

4.   Your acting upon this permission will of course depend upon contingencies, which at present cannot be calculated upon, but one of the first of these, will be the time and place where such permission may reach you; you may be so far on your way South, as to render it too late to retrace your steps with any prospect of your reaching the northern shore this season in time to undertake a search from that quarter and there are other contingencies referred to in the Letter of Sir John Richardson of the 22nd Inst., a copy of which is enclosed.

5.   My Lords have called upon Sir J. Richardson to favor them with his views as to the possible means available to you for such undertaking, and the letter above referred to contains his remarks for your information on this point.

6.   The Hudson's Bay Company have been requested to instruct Mr. Rae, to afford you his best advice and assistance if you should fall in with him; and the Compy. further undertake to deposit provisions at the several points specified in Sir J. Richardson's letter, in order that you may be sure of a supply on your return from the Northward.

7.   With regard to the manner and direction of any search you may make, my Lords would leave it to your judgement and discretion, desiring you to feel assured that should any reasonable objections to such search present themselves their Ldps. would feel no disappointment so far as your conduct is concerned, at your determin-

ing to return with your party to England, and copies of every paper that in the opinion of their Lordships might be of use to you, are herewith enclosed, together with a chart on a large scale, the country near the mouth of the Mackenzie River – and in conclusion I am commanded to convey to you the expression of their Ldps. satisfaction at the report of your conduct up to the date of your departure for the Mackenzie River; and as a further mark of their approval my Lords have been pleased this day to promote you to the rank of Commander, and your commission is herewith enclosed. You will convey to Acting Lieut. Hooper the same expression of the Ldps. satisfaction at the report of his conduct, acquainting him that should he continue to merit your approbation his acting commission as Lieutenant will be confirmed on his passing his examination on his return to England.

Commander Pullen   W.A.B. Hamilton.

APPENDIX ELEVEN

P.R.O., Adm.7/189. *Letter from Lady Franklin to Captain W.A.B. Hamilton, R.N., Second Secretary to the Admiralty, on the promotion of Commander Moore and Lieutenant Pullen.*

January, 1850.

Dear Captain Hamilton,
When I see in detail the just effort which must have been made by Captain Moore to accomplish all he has done, which is really more than would have been expected, it makes me very anxious to know whether he will at once meet with his due reward by promotion. Is it possible for me to do anything, or might I not rather be doing mischief by attempting it? Yet, I feel that I am bound not only by generosity, but in common gratitude to interest myself for the welfare of those who are so nobly serving us.

With regard to Lieutenant Pullen, I have known him of old. He has been in that field of action which brings out all the best energies of a man – he was in S. Australia when I was paying a visit there to Col. & Mrs. Gawlor. His daring and skilful feat in crossing the dangerous bar of the Murray was only one of the many things which make me feel unbounded confidence in him. How very glad I should be to hear of his promotion too. It would be

221

such an encouragement to others as well as himself. I am sure you will be kind enough to tell me if you think I can do anything.

> Believe me dear Captain Hamilton,
> Yours very truly, Jane Franklin.

APPENDIX TWELVE

P.R.O., Adm.7/191. *Commander Pullen to Dr. Rae, 28 June 1850.*

> Great Slave Lake,
> June 28th 1850.

Sir,

I have the honour to request that a passage may be found to York Factory and thence to England by the Company's annual ship for the two persons named in the margin, invalids from the boat expedition, Mr. J. Abernethy, acting 2nd master, J. Senior, Captain F. Top under my command. Also that you will take measures for their being supplied with the undermentioned articles at York Factory.

Mr. Abernethy.	1 pair English shoes.
	1 blk silk handkerchief.
	3 lbs tobacco.
	1 cotton shirt (fine).
	2 lbs yellow soap.
John Senior.	3 lbs tobacco.
	2 lbs yellow soap.

> I have the honour to be,
> Sir,
> Your obedient servant,
> W.J.S. Pullen,
> Commander, R.N.

To:
J. Rae, Esq.,
Chief Factor, H.B.C.S.
In charge of Mackenzie River District.

APPENDIX THIRTEEN

Some notes on York Boats. See also "York Boats," The Beaver, *March 1949, pp 19-23.*

The York Boat was the chief means of transportation along the trade routes of the Hudson's Bay Company from the eighteenth to the twentieth centuries. They were used on the Red, Saskatchewan and Mackenzie Rivers, on Lake Winnipeg and from there to York Factory. Originally they were known as "Inland Boats," eventually taking their well known name from York Factory.

This type of craft was designed to meet the need for a boat that could be built locally and easily, draw little water and was also a good cargo carrier. It had to be seaworthy, and handled under oars or sail, could be portaged and yet required a small crew. The design was most likely influenced by the many Orkneymen who were employed by the Hudson's Bay Company in the eighteenth century. It was a double ended boat with well raked stem and stern posts, a good beam and shallow draft. The length varied between about 28 and 40 feet. The larger boats had a crew of ten men – a coxswain, eight oarsmen and a bowman. A large square sail could be hoisted on a mast stepped about midway between bow and stern. Under sail a rudder was used, while under oars a large sweep or steering oar took its place. The normal cargo was seventy pieces of 90 lbs. each. Later on the bigger York Boats carried one hundred and twenty pieces of 100 lbs. each.

In September 1953, the following details were obtained from a York Boat that was lying inside Fort Garry on the Red River.

Length, overall	40 feet.
Length of keel	30 feet 5½ inches.
Beam	10 feet 6 inches.
Depth	3 feet 1½ inches.
Rake of stem post	35°
Rake of stern post	50°

This boat had eight planks a side. The top two were planked clinker fashion, the remainder carvel fashion. She was fitted to pull four oars each side.

Bibliography

Adney & Chapelle. *The Bark Canoe and Skin Boats of North America.* Washington, Smithsonian Institution, 1964.

Armstrong, Alex. *A personal narrative of the discovery of the North-West Passage . . . during nearly five years continuous service in the Arctic Regions while in search of the Arctic expedition under Sir John Franklin.* London; Hurst & Blackett; 1857.

Baird, P.D. "Expeditions to the Canadian Arctic." *The Beaver,* March, June and September 1949.

Bredin, T.F. " 'Whale Island' and the Mackenzie Delta: Charted Errors and Unmapped Discoveries, 1789 to 1850." *Arctic,* Journal of the Arctic Institute of North America, Vol. 15, No. 1, 1962.

Collinson, R. *Journal of H.M.S. Enterprise, on the expedition in search of Sir John Franklin's ships by Behring's Strait (1850-55).* London; Sampson, Low; 1889.

Dodge, E.S. *Northwest by Sea.* New York, Oxford University Press, 1961.

Durham, Bill. *Canoes and Kayaks of Western America.* Seattle, Copper Canoe Press, 1960.

Franklin, J. *Narrative of a Journey to the Shores of the Polar Sea in the years 1819-20-21-22,* Vols. I & II. London, John Murray, 1824.

Franklin, J. *Narrative of a second expedition to the shores of the Polar Sea, in the years 1825, 1826 and 1827.* London, John Murray, 1828.

Gilpin, J.D. *Outline of the Voyage of H.M.S. Enterprize and Investigator to Bar-*

row Strait in search of Sir John Franklin. London, The Nautical Magazine, 1850.

Hooper, W.H. *Ten Months among the Tents of the Tuski.* London, John Murray, 1853.

Hudson's Bay Company. *The Beaver:* March 1934, "The ship 'Prince of Wales' "; December 1943, "The La Loche Brigade"; March & June 1947, "Pullen in search of Franklin"; March 1949, "York Boats"; Spring 1955, "Halkett's Air Boat."

Hudson's Bay Record Society. Vol. XVI, *Rae's Arctic Correspondence, 1844-55.* London, The Hudson's Bay Record Society, 1953.

M'Clure, R.M. *The discovery of the North-West Passage by H.M.S. Investigator, Captain R.M. M'Clure, 1850, 1851, 1852, 1853, 1854.* Edited by Commander Sherard Osborn, London, Longmans; 1856.

Mackay, J. Ross. *The Mackenzie Delta, N.W.T.* Department of Mines and Technical Surveys, Geographical Branch, Minute 8, Ottawa. The Queen's Printer, 1963.

Mariner's Mirror. Vol. 44, 1958. No. 2. "The Halkett Boat and other portable boats."

Morse, E.W. *Fur Trade Canoe Routes of Canada/Then and Now.* Ottawa, The Queen's Printer, 1969.

Neatby, L.H. *Frozen Ships: The Arctic Diary of Johann Miertsching, 1850–1854.* Toronto, Macmillan of Canada, 1967.

Parliamentary Papers. 1847-48. Vol. XLI, Paper 264, Paper 386.
1850. Vol. XXXV, Paper 107.
1851. Vol. XXXIII, Paper 97.
1852. Vol. L, Paper 1449.

Poulson, N. *The White Ribbon.* London, B.A. Seaby, Ltd., 1968. (This book contains the Medal Roll for all Arctic and Polar Medals from 1818 to 1966.)

Public Record Office. Adm. 2/1608. Admiralty orders of 25 January 1850 to Commander Pullen.

Adm. 7/189. Report of Proceedings of H.M.S. *Plover*, 25 September 1849.

Adm. 7/189. Dr. Rae to Sir John Richardson, 5 October 1849.

Adm. 7/189. Report of Proceedings of H.M.S. *Herald*, 22 November 1849.

Adm. 7/189. Commander T.E.L. Moore's orders to Lieutenant Pullen, 25 July 1849.

Adm. 7/189. Captain H. Kellett's instructions to Lieutenant Pullen, 25 July 1849.

Adm. 7/189. Lady Franklin to Captain W.A.B. Hamilton on the promotion of Commander Moore and Lieutenant Pullen, January 1850.

Adm. 7/191. Commander Pullen to Dr. Rae, 28 June 1850.

Adm. 38/2041. Muster List of H.M.S. *Crocodile*, October 1851.

Pullen, W.J.S. *MS, Narrative by Vice Admiral W.J.S. Pullen.* Public Library, Museum and Art Gallery of South Australia.

Richardson, Sir J. *Arctic Searching Expedition.* New York, Harper and Brothers, 1852.

Sanderson, M.W.B. *Voyages and Travel.* London, H.M. Stationery Office, 1968.

Seemann, B.C. *Narrative of the voyage of H.M.S. Herald during the years 1845-51, under the command of Captain Henry Kellett, R.N., C.B.,* Vols. I & II, London, Reeve & Co., 1853.

Smith, D. Murray. *Arctic Expeditions from British and Foreign Shores from the earliest times to the Expedition of 1875-76.* Glasgow, Melbourne and Dunedin, M'Gready, Thompson & Niven, 1877.

Wright, N. *Quest for Franklin.* London, Melbourne, Toronto, Heinemann, 1959.

ABBREVIATIONS

D.N.B.   Dictionary of National Biography.

H.B.R.S. Hudson's Bay Record Society.

P.P.   Parliamentary Papers. (Great Britain: House of Commons' command papers relating to the Franklin Search Expeditions.), H.M. Stationery Office.

P.R.O.   Public Record Office.

Index

DATE DUE   ECHEANCE